A Boy and His Dog

The Ultimate Handbook for Every Boy Who Cares for His Dog

By Cynthia Copeland

Cider Mill Press
Kennebunkport, Maine

13-Digit ISBN: 978-1-60433-058-8
10-Digit ISBN: 1-60433-058-9

This book may be ordered by mail from the publisher. Please include $2.50 for
postage and handling. Please support your local bookseller first!

Books published by Cider Mill Press Book Publishers are available at special
discounts for bulk purchases in the United States by corporations, institutions,
and other organizations. For more information, please contact the publisher.

Cider Mill Press Book Publishers
"Where good books are ready for press"
12 Port Farm Road
Kennebunkport, Maine 04046

Visit us on the web!
www.cidermillpress.com

Design by Jimmy Ball

Printed in China

1 2 3 4 5 6 7 8 9 0
First Edition

For Quentin, a wonderful boy who loves dogs
(and lizards, and snakes, and turtles, and guinea pigs ...)

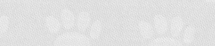

Table of Contents

Introduction

Congratulations On Your New Dog! Whether you bought a purebred dog from a good local breeder or fell in love with a mutt at the shelter, you have a lot to look forward to as you bond with the newest member of your family.

When I was growing up, I had a dog named Dusty (below). He was a border terrier, and had a wiry coat, velvety ears, and a sweet disposition. Dusty had been given to my brothers and me by a librarian in our small town who couldn't care for him anymore.

Each day when I'd come home from school, Dusty would be waiting to greet me by the back kitchen door. He was only allowed on the linoleum floors, but I knew that when I went to my room I'd find a warm spot on my bed where he had been curled up until he heard our car in the driveway.

Dusty was smart, and he was usually well behaved, but that was mostly because he held out hope that at any minute he might be given a Dog Yummy treat.

Dusty with my brother Gary, 1972

He loved those treats more than he loved us. (One time I dared my brother John to eat a Dog Yummy. He did, and I paid him a dollar. But that didn't solve the mystery of why Dusty was so crazy about them, because John said it tasted like dirt.)

Like lots of dogs, Dusty enjoyed smelling as awful as possible. He was especially fond of rolling in a patch of skunk cabbage on the edge of our lawn. My brothers and I would play rock-paper-scissors to determine who had to give him a bath after each of these episodes. (Because my littlest brother was only five and always put out "rock," he lost every time.)

Even though he was stinky, Dusty was always willing to be whatever we needed him to be: a pillow, a footstool, a handkerchief, a wrestling partner, or a playmate.

I'll never forget Dusty, and you'll never forget your first dog, either. I hope this book will help you develop a great relationship with your dog—one that is rewarding and fun for you both.

Dog Notes

My name is _____

and I am _____ years old.

These are some things I want to remember about my dog:

I got my dog on (date) _____

from_____.

I named my dog _____ because _____

_____.

The funniest thing he ever did was_____

_____

_____.

His favorite person is_____.

The grossest thing he ever ate was_____

_____.

His favorite thing to do is _____

_____.

His favorite place to sleep is _____

_____.

His best trick is _____

_____.

If he could only have one toy, he would choose_____

_____.

His favorite thing to eat is _____

_____.

If he were a person, he would be just like _____

because _____.

My dog is the (circle one) jock/nerd/class clown/class president/

social reject of the dog world because _____

_____.

The thing I'll never forget about my dog is _____

_____

_____.

Wait Till You Hear What My Dog Does ...

Boys and dogs are meant for each other. And boys have a way of noticing, well, everything about their dogs. Even, or maybe especially, pretty gross stuff. And some of it's just funny. Or weird. Or even cool.

When asked what odd quirks their dogs have, here's what some real boys had to say:

"My dog loves crayons. I can always tell which poops belong to my dog because they are really colorful."

—Josh

"Dusty, my golden retriever, will take one shoe from every pair and add it to a little shoe pile in his bed that he uses as a pillow."

—Ben

"My dog refuses to eat the leftovers on my plate, but then he'll go outside and eat a slug or a couple of pebbles. His taste buds are really weird."

—Michael

"Dixie drinks her water so fast that she throws it up. If we burp her like a baby after she drinks, though, she's OK. If anyone in the family hears her lapping up her water, we run

like crazy to burp her so we don't have to clean up a mess."
—Gabe

"My dog loves to go through the wastebaskets in the house. One time, she got my baby sister's diaper stuck to her head and came running through the house all freaked out!"
—Mack

"We don't have a doorbell. We have NEVER had a doorbell. And yet when someone rings a doorbell on a TV show, my dog goes running over to the front door barking like crazy!"
—Nicholas

"Zeke runs to the end of a street, stops … and turns right. Always right, never left. The good news is that he never gets lost. After about three right turns, he's back where he started. The bad news is that he's never going to play baseball."
—Henry

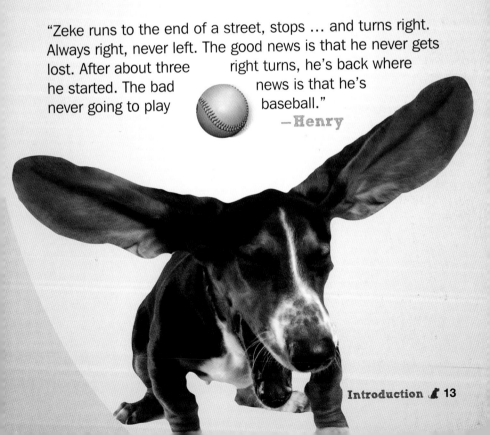

Chapter 1

Naming Your Dog One of the coolest things about owning a dog is that YOU get to name him! (Of course, your little sister, your mother, and the kid down the street will make lots of suggestions!)

Over the years, dogs were often named after traits. A Dalmatian, for example, might be called Spot. Nowadays, human names like Max and Molly are popular. People also seem to like names that make their pets sound smart, like Wallace or Miles. Here are today's most popular dog names:

For Boy Dogs ...

1. **Max**
2. Jake
3. Buddy
4. Bailey
5. **Sam**
6. Rocky
7. bUSteR
8. Casey
9. **Cody**
10. DUKE

For Girl Dogs ...

1. Maggie
2. Molly
3. Lady
4. **Sadie**
5. Lucy
6. Daisy
7. Ginger
8. ABBY
9. Sasha
10. *Sandy*

Here are some common dog names in other parts of the world:

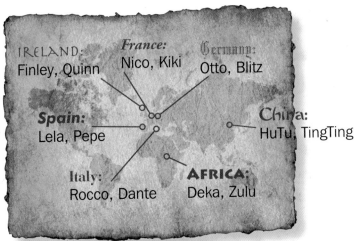

IRELAND:
Finley, Quinn

France:
Nico, Kiki

Germany:
Otto, Blitz

Spain:
Lela, Pepe

China:
HuTu, TingTing

Italy:
Rocco, Dante

AFRICA:
Deka, Zulu

If you don't want to pick a "regular" name, how about naming your pup after a Disney dog? You have lots of choices from *101 Dalmatians* (like Pongo or Perdita), or you could choose Goofy, Pluto, Tramp, Bruno, or Nana. If you plan on spending lots of time in front of the tube with your pooch, you may want to name him after a famous TV dog. How about Astro (*The Jetsons*), Mr. Peabody (*Rocky & Bullwinkle*), Comet (*Full House*), or Lassie (*Lassie*)?

If you think you might want to be the president of the United States someday, you may want to get a head start and name your dog after a president's dog. George Washington had Mopsey, Captain, and Vulcan. Fido and Jip were Abraham Lincoln's dogs. Some presidents chose very odd names for their dogs, like King Tut and Weejie (Herbert Hoover's dogs), or Winks and Tiny (Franklin Roosevelt's dogs). For lots of other ideas, check out *www.alldognames.com*.

Weird Dog Fact
Dogs that have been raised solely by humans without other dogs do not wag their tails nearly as much as typical dogs.

Your parents had to worry about certain things when they named you. You *don't* have to worry about these things when you name your dog:

1. You don't have to worry that other dogs will give yours a dumb nickname.

2. You don't have to worry whether or not your dog will end up with weird initials.

3. You don't have to worry that the teachers will mispronounce your dog's name on the first day of school every year.

4. You don't have to worry that your dog will be assigned to the wrong cabin at summer camp because no one can tell by his name whether he's a boy or a girl.

5. You don't have to worry about your parents being upset that you didn't name your dog after them.

Doggy Tip

Use your dog's name only when you're happy with him. Never use it when you're angry. "Good dog, Lassie!" is perfect; "NO, NO, BAD DOG, BUDDY!" is not. When you need to say *no*, say it (don't shout it) just once.

Here are some real, true things you *do* have to worry about when you name your dog:

1. Select a name that doesn't sound too much like a command. "Moe," for instance, sounds too much like "no." Once you see the pattern, you will understand why Fletch or May would not be great choices, either.

2. If you have a sister named Lilly and a brother named Willy, you won't want to name your dog Millie. Dogs get confused easily. The poor thing won't know if your mother is telling her to set the table, take out the garbage, or sit and stay.

3. Make sure the name you choose will be easy for the puppy to remember. Two-syllable names are best. Save the name Cleopatra for your cat, who will never come when you call her anyway, so it doesn't really matter.

4. Think about what the name sounds like when you are yelling it across the park. "Come, Jack!" might sound better than "Come, Fuzzy Wuzzy!" And because we're talking about yelling a name in the park, you might want to choose a name that is not super-popular. If you call "Max!" you may end up bringing three Maxes home with you, none of them being your own Max.

Teaching Your Puppy His Name

Teaching a puppy his name is easy. First, with the puppy near you, say the name loudly and happily—"Rover!"—and give him a treat each time you say it. Do this a number of times throughout the day.

Next, try it with him a little farther away. In a happy, enthusiastic voice, say "Rover, come!" Each time he comes to you when you call him, give him a treat. Repeat this often!

Changing Your Dog's Name

If you get a dog already named Jake and you have your heart set on Cody, don't worry. You can teach the dog a new name. At first, call the dog by the name Jake and give him a treat for coming. In a few days, begin calling him by both names, starting with Cody, his new name. Call "Cody Jake!" and reward him when he comes. A week later, try dropping the name Jake, and just use Cody. Reward him with praise and a treat when he comes.

You should not change the dog's name more than once because he will get mixed up. Imagine how hard it would be for you if your parents suddenly decided to call you "Albert"! It might take a little getting used to!

Weird Dog Fact
Walt Disney's family dog was a poodle named Lady.

TOP TEN Coolest Web Sites for Boys and Dogs

Surf the web to learn interesting facts about dogs, find cool stuff to buy for your dog, or watch silly dogs in action!

www.loveyourdog.com

This great site is entitled "A Kid's Guide to Dog Care." It offers loads of tips on care, training, and fun things to do with your dog, as well as areas where kids can share stories, photos, and more about their dogs!

www.aspca.org

On the official web site for the American Society for the Prevention of Cruelty to Animals, you'll find great tips for dog care, answers to animal questions of all kinds, cartoons, and more.

www.akc.org/kids_juniors

Check out the site of the American Kennel Club, which oversees thousands of dog events all over the country and is the world's largest registry of purebred dogs. The site has all sorts of information about dog breeds, dog care, fun activities you can do with your dog, and even things kids can do to help educate people about responsible dog ownership.

www.petfinder.com

This excellent site, which matches thousands of homeless pets with new owners, offers lots of neat stuff about dogs. Just click on "Fun" on the home page, and you'll find games, funny pet videos, and tips on traveling with your dog. Click on "Training" for a great selection of step-by-step video clips that show you how to teach your dog a whole bunch of things—from walking on a leash to playing hide and seek! It also is a great place to learn about how to volunteer or raise money to help homeless animals.

www.thirteen.org/extraordinarydogs

The PBS television show *Nature* went in search of extraordinary dogs. On this site, you can read fun facts, jokes, and stories of amazing dogs.

www.workingdogweb.com/Kids&Dogs.htm

Here you'll find fun links to dog-related projects, games, stories, favorite dog cartoons, and more!

www.canismajor.com/dog

You'll learn lots of great information about living with dogs, and find a list of books and videos that can help you learn about all kinds of canine training and activities.

www.sillydogs.net

See a dog being brushed until he looks like a lion, and another pup that plays chess!

www.dogchannel.com

From dog training to dog care, activities to events, this site has all the info you need to raise a perfect pooch.

www.dogoftheday.com

Proud of your pup? Nominate him to be Dog of the Day! You can read all about other people's great dogs and chat with other dog lovers!

Chapter 2

Bringing Your Dog Home the big day is coming! If you are going to be picking up a puppy, you'll need to wait until he is at least 8 weeks old before it's OK to separate him from his mother, brothers, and sisters. If you are adopting an older dog, you may have just a few days to get ready while your local shelter or purebred rescue completes the paperwork. Rather than just X-ing off days on your calendar, there are lots of things you can do to prepare for his homecoming.

First of all, you'll want to act like a dog! Get down on your hands and knees, and see what your new dog will be able to get into when he comes to your house. Are there cords he can chew on, household cleaners that might poison him, trash baskets just at chin level for him to search, a dish of chocolate treats within reach?

If you have chairs with wooden legs, watch out! Puppies, especially, love to chew on chair legs! You'll have to dog-proof your house just like new parents baby-proof their house.

Decide with your parents what room the dog will be confined to at first. You'll want it to be a place where he won't be alone—and where, if he makes a mess, it'll be easy to clean up. The kitchen is a good choice.

When you are home and watching him, you can let him explore other parts of the house, but until he is older and more settled, you'll want to confine him the rest of the time.

Even an older dog that is housebroken should have a limited area to roam at first. You don't know the dog yet, and he doesn't know you or your house. It'll take a little time for you to find out if he has any bad habits you need to address.

Most dogs love to run and play, and all dogs need some exercise. So you'll need to make arrangements to give your dog the chance to romp outdoors. But dogs do best when they can spend most of their time with people, not left alone outside for long periods. Dogs are very social animals— they want to be with their human companions! When they're tied up outside by themselves, they're unhappy, and that can cause bad behavior.

If you have a fenced-in yard that allows you to play safely with your dog, great! If not, your dog might like a "dog run"—a cable that attaches between two trees, with a leash that slides along it. That will allow him to play with you without getting tangled or running away. Some dog owners have had good luck with electric fences. And some dogs—especially small or medium-sized ones—get plenty of exercise simply by being taken on a nice walk with their owners a few times a day.

Pup Quiz

The average annual cost of owning a dog, which includes basic needs such as food, veterinary care, grooming and boarding, is:

a. $328

b. $878

c. $1,571

d. $2,344

What Will It Be Like When My Dog Comes Home?

The hardest part of anything new is that often it's very different from what you imagined. You may be thinking that when you have your new dog, she'll follow you everywhere and sleep by your side and quickly learn all sorts of neat tricks. In reality, if she's a young puppy, she may be scared for the first few days and cry a lot. She won't be able to sleep in your bed because she won't be housebroken yet. She'll need a lot of rest. You shouldn't drag her along everywhere you go. It will be a few months before you can begin teaching her tricks.

Answer: c. $1,571

Continued on page 28

Here's what you'll need to buy before your dog comes home:

baby gate(s)
a great way to keep the dog confined to a certain area of the house

a crate
for safety and housetraining (for more about this, see chapter 4)

a collar
a buckle-style collar that is large enough for two of your fingers to fit between the dog's neck and the collar, but small enough so that it won't slip over his head

a dog tag
with your dog's name and your phone number printed on it, so that he will be returned to you if he ever gets lost

As your dog grows, remember to check that his collar hasn't become too tight! You should always be able to easily slip two fingers under it.

leashes

a short one for everyday walks and in-house training, and a longer one for outdoor romps

food and treats

it's best to start out with the same food that he's been eating

bowls for food and water

heavy, stainless steel bowls that are easy to clean and hard to tip over

a dog bed

with a zip-off cover for washing, and big enough for him when he's grown

a dog brush and other grooming supplies

chosen with your dog's coat in mind

toys

for chewing, fetching, and playing

You can cut down on costs by making a few items rather than buying them. For a dog bed, have your mom or dad help you cut a cardboard box to make it easy for the pup to go in and out. Put an old towel in the bottom. Rather than buy toys, see page 123 for ideas on making your own toys. You could also help your parents hunt for bargains—you might find a crate, baby gate, and bowls at yard sales or thrift stores.

That's not to say that she won't be sweet and cuddly right away, but she will demand a lot from you. All of a sudden, you will have to think of what your dog needs, not just what you need. Maybe you won't be able to watch your favorite TV show because she needs to be walked.

Remember that this is a relationship, just like the relationships you have with your friends. It takes a while to figure out what a new kid is like and how to make a friendship work, and it's the same with your new dog. You'll work everything out over time—if you have realistic expectations, that is. If you understand that it won't be perfect from the start, then you will be better able to handle the first few weeks.

DOGGY TIP

The day before you pick up your puppy, call the breeder. Ask him to put a hand towel or rag in with all of the puppies.

When you get your puppy, take the rag home, too, and put it in your puppy's bed so that he will have something that smells familiar.

How To Pick Up A Puppy

To safely pick up your puppy, wait until she is standing. Put one hand under her chest and one under her bottom so that your arms are outside of her four legs. Pick up the puppy so that she doesn't tip forward or backward, and snuggle her to your chest so that she feels secure.

The Ride Home

You've probably imagined the car ride home with the puppy snuggled on your lap, looking up at you adoringly from time to time. In fact, the ride may not be like that at all! The puppy may get carsick, cry nonstop, or pee everywhere. No problem—as long as you're prepared! The best idea is to bring a box for the puppy to travel in. You can line it

> The dog was created especially for children. He is the god of frolic.
>
> —**Henry Ward Beecher**

DOGGY TIP

Have plenty of safe chew toys on hand before you bring home your new dog or puppy!

Puppies—and even some older dogs—love to chew and will appreciate toys that are meant especially for them. An old, clean washcloth that you've soaked in water and then frozen works well. Gnawing on it will make your pup's gums feel better, and will make him less likely to chew on your boots or gloves! Spraying Bitter Apple (available at pet stores) or sprinkling cayenne pepper on things you don't want him to chew will discourage him.

with newspapers and an old towel. Have paper towels with you in case you have messes to clean up elsewhere in the car.

Ask your mom or dad to drive slowly and smoothly so the pup isn't startled. Speak softly and calmly to him. If you can stand it, have your mom or dad play classical music quietly on the radio.

One important note: The first thing to do when you get your puppy is to put on his collar and tags. That way, you're prepared in case the unthinkable happens and he darts away from you.

The First Day

As hard as it will be, don't have all of your friends waiting at your house to see the new puppy. You'll have lots of time to show her off once she's used to her home and family.

Remind your brothers and sisters to stay quiet and calm around the new puppy. They should sit on the floor and let her come to them rather than running after her. Unless they are old enough to do it right (see the picture on page 28), they shouldn't try to pick her up.

Bring the puppy into the room that you set apart with gates. Let her explore, sniffing and roaming about. She may piddle here or there, but let it go for now. You want her to feel that her new home is a happy, safe place. You can worry about housetraining later.

It's hard to know how your particular pup will respond on the first day. She may be nervous and shy, or outgoing and adventurous. It depends on her personality. Just don't be upset if things don't happen exactly as you had planned. She may fall asleep rather

My Dog Story

"When we first got our puppy—MY puppy!—he would only go to my mom! That totally bummed me out. Then my dad rubbed some butter on my hand and told me to hold it out to Benji and let him lick my hand, and he would like me better. It worked!"

—Mack

Your other pets may not be as happy about the new dog as you are! Older, bigger dogs may try to show the new pup who's in charge. That's natural. In packs, dogs quickly figure out who's the boss and who's not.

Even though it will be hard to do, pay more attention to the dog you've had in the family for a long time. That will make him feel more secure and will help him work things out with the puppy.

Cats will usually find their own hiding places in the house until they feel comfortable with the new dog. If that's not possible, you can keep the two animals separated until the pooch has settled in.

My Dog Story

"I was only four when we got our puppy, and I insisted that we name him 'Casper the Friendly Ghost' because I had been watching a bunch of those cartoons. I'm 10 now, so I just call him 'Cass.' I hate taking him to the vet because they always call him by his full name, and it's pretty embarrassing."

–Willy

than wanting to play with you, or she may prefer being with your sister rather than you. It's all about the dog getting used to your family, and all of you getting used to her.

Begin your crate-training right away by feeding her in her crate and gently encouraging her to go in and out of it. (See Chapter 4 for more information on using the crate.)

The First Week

Even with your mom or dad's help, taking care of your new dog is not easy. Sometimes it might feel like you've taken on too much. Don't worry—things get much easier with every passing day. The dog will get used to you and your house rules, and you'll understand her better and know what she needs. Like any relationship, it just takes a little time.

You'll learn that you can't leave shoes near the puppy or she will chew them. You'll learn that the puppy whines and barks when you put her in the crate, but only for a few minutes, then she goes to sleep. You'll learn that she needs to go outside as soon as she wakes up, and a few minutes after she's had a drink of water, or eaten, or played. You'll learn about the puppy and she'll learn about you and living in your house.

In the first week, you can begin to teach the puppy her name. You can reward her with a Cheerio or another small treat if she comes to you when you say her name. Get the puppy used to spending short periods of time in her crate. Show her the outside spot where she should pee and poop. Get her used to the leash by attaching it to her collar and letting her drag it around the house. Don't tug and jerk her around with it! But watch her closely to make sure the leash doesn't get caught on something and choke her.

Show her the stairs—you can hold her belly and gently encourage her if she's scared. You'll have to watch her all the time to make sure she doesn't get into something that could hurt her. The following chapters have information about all of these things.

My Dog Story

"We named our black lab puppy 'Pucky' when we first got him because he looked like a hockey puck. But then he threw up the first time we took him in the car, so we started calling him 'Pukey.' "

–Henry

I bought a dog the other day ... I named him Stay. It's fun to call him: "Come here, Stay! Come here, Stay!" He went insane.

–Comedian Steven Wright

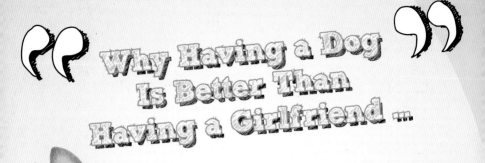

" Why Having a Dog Is Better Than Having a Girlfriend ... "

🦴 Your dog doesn't care if you pay attention to another dog.

🦴 Your dog doesn't care if you forget her birthday. (Hey, she probably forgot it, too).

🦴 Your dog doesn't tell you that your friends are gross.

🦴 Your dog doesn't remember every dumb little thing you ever did.

💀 Your dog doesn't care if you fart or burp.

💀 **Your dog agrees with you that cats are dumb.**

💀 You and your dog can pass a happy afternoon together watching lame TV shows and scratching yourselves (and your dog lets you control the TV remote).

💀 **Your dog doesn't care if you drink out of the milk carton—hey, he drinks out of the toilet.**

Chapter 3

Feeding and Watering There are so many choices in the dog food aisle. How will your family decide what to feed your dog?

In the beginning, he should be fed whatever he's been eating at the breeder, shelter, or other home. Your dog will be a little nervous about coming to your house, so you'll want to make things as familiar as you can. (Imagine what you would want if you were going to be visiting your grandparents for a long time. You'd want to open the refrigerator and find all your favorite snacks and drinks!)

When he's settled in and it's time to change dog food (from puppy to adult food, for instance), do it a little at a time. Mix the old and the new food together for a while until you think he's used to the change. A sudden switch might upset his stomach.

As for what kind of food he should eat, you'll notice that labels on the food bags indicate if the food is for puppies, older dogs, overweight dogs, active dogs, and more. You can help your mom or dad pick out a high-quality, brand-name dog food that is specially made for your dog's age and activity level.

Weird Dog Fact
If your dog is eating a balanced diet, he should make from one to four solid, odor-free poops a day. Young dogs poop a lot more often than adults!

Yum It Up
If your dog refuses to eat his dry dog food, drizzle it with low-salt chicken broth. He'll think it's a whole new kind of food!

Dinner Time

Most vets say that feeding more than one meal a day works best for most dogs. You can read the label on the dog food bag for an idea of how much food to put out at each meal. (Dry food, also called kibble, is considered by some to be better for dogs than canned or "wet" food because it helps keep their teeth clean.) Your dog's age will help determine how often you should feed him. In general, young puppies should eat at least three times a day. When he's three or four months old, you can switch to twice a day. Try to feed your dog at about the same times every day—this will help a lot with housetraining.

Weird Dog Fact
Every year, Americans spend $1.5 billion on pet food.

Treats

Treats are like dessert for your dog. From Milk Bone® dog biscuits to pigs' ears, there are all sorts of goodies you can offer your pup when he's been a good fella. Don't overdo, though, or you'll end up with a pudgy puppy! It might be a good idea to save treats for training rewards.

Treats You Can Make Yourself

If you'd like to try cooking for your dog, here are some great recipes from Jessica Disbrow Talley, author of *The Organic Dog Biscuit Cookbook* and co-owner of the Bubba Rose Biscuit Company dog treat bakery.

These treats power up your pup for a whole day of digging, fetching, and jumping.

1¼ c. oat flour*

1¼ c. brown rice flour*

½ c. rolled oats (the old-fashioned kind, not instant)

½ c. granola (cannot contain raisins)

1 egg

¼ c. molasses (blackstrap or regular)

⅔ c. water

*All-purpose flour or whole wheat flour may be used instead of oat flour or brown rice flour.

Preheat the oven to 350°. Combine all the ingredients together and mix them thoroughly. Roll the dough into small balls (about 1" in diameter) and place them on an ungreased cookie sheet. (They can be rather close together, as they don't spread while cooking.) Press each one down with your hand to flatten the cookies.

Bake for 18 to 22 minutes or until the edges are golden brown. Let them cool completely on a wire rack. Store them at room temperature in a loosely covered container.

Ever consider what dogs must think of us? I mean, here we come back from a grocery store with the most amazing haul—chicken, pork, half a cow. They must think we're the greatest hunters on Earth!

—Anne Tyler

These biscuits are favorites of dogs and their owners (although in general it's best not to taste-test your dog's treats, even on a dare).

1½ c. oat flour*

1½ c. brown rice flour*

1 c. shredded low-fat cheddar cheese

½ c. grated parmesan cheese

1 egg

1 c. water

*All-purpose flour or whole wheat flour may be used instead of oat flour or brown rice flour.

Preheat the oven to 350°. Combine all the ingredients and mix thoroughly until a dough forms. Roll the dough out on a lightly floured surface to ¼" thickness. Use a cookie cutter to cut out shapes. Place the biscuits on an ungreased cookie sheet. (They can be close together as they don't spread much while cooking.)

Bake for 20 to 25 minutes or until the biscuits are golden brown. Remove them from the oven and let them cool completely on a wire rack. Store the treats in an airtight container in the refrigerator.

My Dog Story

"When I take my dog for a hike, I make dog trail mix to bring along. In a baggie, I mix together Cheerios® or Kix® cereal, dry dog food, and some treats broken into little pieces. If I let him off of the leash, I call him and them give him some trail mix as a reward for coming."

—Adam

Water

Your dog needs to be able to drink clean water whenever he's thirsty. You don't want to limit his water intake. This is especially important in warm weather!

If he eats dry food, he'll need more water than if he eats wet food. Every time you take a drink, check to see if your dog's bowl needs refilling.

The only exception to this is when you are housebreaking him: take his dish away about two hours before bedtime. That way he won't need to pee in the middle of the night.

DOGGY TIP

The ASPCA (The American Society for the Prevention of Cruelty to Animals) supports a poison-control hotline for animals that is open 24 hours a day. Call 888-426-4435.

The organization may need to charge a consultation fee (using a credit card) for the call; be sure to ask about that first.

No Bones About It

Did you know that it's not always a good idea to give your dog a bone? A raw bone from the grocer that has been refrigerated is OK for your dog to chew on for a few hours, but it should then be thrown out, as it may spoil. And cooked bones of any type are a big no-no—your dog chews up and swallows small pieces that end up as very sharp, indigestible objects in the intestinal tract. This can cause your dog serious problems! If you're not sure, ask your vet if a type of bone is OK.

"Treats" to Avoid

You may be surprised to learn that some foods people love can be poisonous to dogs. Here are some of the "treats" you never want to give your pup:

Raisins

Grapes

Garlic

Onions

Chocolate

Coffee

Tea

Colas

Avocado

Mushrooms

Macadamia Nuts

Alcohol

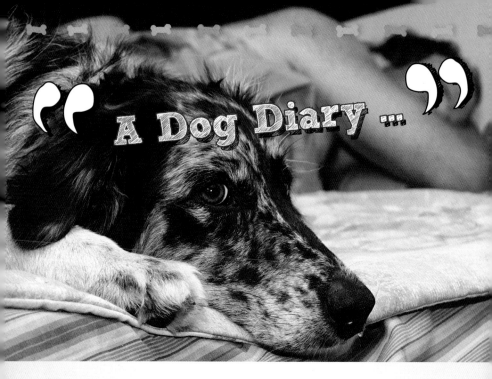

"A Dog Diary ..."

5:00 A.M. Yay! Yippee! The sun is up!

5:23 A.M. I finally woke everyone else up! WEEE-HAA!

6:39 A.M. WOW! Dog food! YUM!! I LOVE that stuff! So dry and crunchy!

8:45 A.M. Yowza! We're going for a WALK! Walks are the best!

10:08 A.M. I chased my tail and almost caught it!

11:17 A.M. A ride in the car?! WOW! How lucky can a dog get?! Window nose-prints!!

1:49 P.M. MORE dog food?! Golly! This is my lucky day!

3:29 P.M. The kids are home! Yea! Someone might pat me! Someone might even rub my BELLY!!

4:13 P.M. Fresh water in my dish! Man! How great is that?!

5:50 P.M. LEFTOVERS?! —I mean, can this day get any better?!

6:28 P.M. ANOTHER WALK? How great is MY life?! And we're headed for the PARK where I might even get to sniff another dog!

8:45 P.M. Seriously? I can sleep on your bed?! This is unbelievable! Life is FANTASTIC!!

Chapter 4

Housebreaking If you've already cleaned up a few messes in the house, you may be feeling a bit frustrated. Not to worry. Your puppy can be housebroken, it's just going to take a little time and a good game plan.

* keeping him in his crate or another confined space when you can't be watching him

* knowing when he'll have to "go"

* feeding him healthy food at the same times every day

* taking him outside often so that he has lots of opportunities to "go"

* teaching him to pee or poop at your command

* learning the right way to correct him when he makes a mess in the house

Ideas about housebreaking have changed in the past several years. Experts no longer tell dog owners to stick a dog's face in his mess and scold him—now trainers realize that this will only confuse your pup and damage his trust in you. Using a crate is a relatively recent idea, too. You may need to respectfully teach other family members the new and improved way of "taking care of business."

The important thing to remember when training your dog to pee and poop outside is that dogs want to please you, and will do whatever gets them positive attention from you. (Later on, you'll see how this works when teaching them tricks!)

So you want to be sure to heap praise and attention on your pooch when he does something right. That's the only way he can understand what you want—and it will make him want to repeat it!

Another thing to consider is your dog's personality. Some dogs are eager to please, while others are more laid-back or timid. An important thing with dogs—as well as with people!—is to figure out what motivates them. What will make your dog want to do what you are telling him to? Is it food? Praise? Play time? Whether you want him to poop in a certain spot or stay off the furniture, you need to know what is important to him so that you can reward him with something he wants!

Crate Training

Crate training may seem like a mean thing to do, but it's not! It's like putting a toddler in a playpen—used in the right way, it keeps him safe when there is no one to watch him closely. And, in the case of both a toddler and a dog, it keeps the house safe from them, too!

What Is Praise?

Praise means looking at your puppy and speaking to him in a happy, upbeat tone of voice. It can work especially well when you give him a food treat at the same time. When you praise your dog, you should be standing, looking down at him. You don't want to get him so excited by jumping about and shouting that he can't pay attention to you.

The reason that crate training works in housebreaking is that dogs do not want to pee or poop in the same place that they sleep. It's an instinct left over from their days in the wild, when a soiled den might make animals sick.

The crate is not used just for housebreaking, it is also helpful when you will be out of the house for a few hours, or at night.

If you and your family introduce the crate the right way, most dogs will come to accept it. Give your pup a treat in the crate, and praise him when he goes inside. At first, let him spend a short time in it with the door open. Gradually work toward having him stay inside for longer periods. Many dogs will go into their crates, which they see as their dens, without even being told to—especially if there is a lot of excitement and they want a little peace and quiet. The important thing is to use the crate appropriately so that the dog doesn't mind being crated.

Buying a Crate

Pet stores offer a wide variety of crates. There are a few things to think about when you buy one:

SIZE: The crate should be big enough so that the dog

Not sure where to put the crate? Your mom or dad can buy a piece of plywood a bit larger than the crate, and set it right on top—instant table!

can stand up and turn around comfortably. It should be small enough that he will not be tempted to poop in one corner and then sleep on the opposite end.

If you have a "Clifford," a tiny puppy that will grow into a big dog, consider borrowing a small crate to start! You don't want to have to buy two crates in a six-month period. The other option is to make some sort of divider in the crate with heavy cardboard or wood. (You can also buy a crate with a built-in divider.) The divider should be movable, so that as the dog grows, you can move it to allow more room. When he's grown, you can take it out altogether.

SAFETY: You want your pup to be safe in his crate. Unless your dad or mom is a carpenter, you probably want to avoid trying to make your own. Homemade ones can have hidden dangers you might not have thought of. Commercially made crates have been tested and proven to be safe.

STYLE: Wire or mesh crates are better in some situations than the hard plastic ones, because they allow more air to flow in and out. The plastic ones are more den-like, but in them the pup can't see what's happening in the room.

PRICE: Crates can be expensive. You could help your mom or dad look for a used one. Check the newspaper's classified ads, ask friends who have older dogs who might not use the crate anymore, or have your parents stop by a few garage sales to see if you can find one.

Setting Up the Crate

You want a combination of cozy and practical when you set up your dog's crate. For the practical side, you can line the bottom with newspapers to make it easier to clean up his "mistakes." For the cozy part, you can find a small blanket or towel for him to rest on. If it's very soft and cushy inside, though, check the bedding often to be sure that it's clean, because some dogs are tempted to pee on those kinds of surfaces.

Put the crate in a corner of the kitchen or in your bedroom. A puppy, especially, won't want to be alone at night. (You can cover the crate with a blanket at night to encourage him to sleep.) During the day, he should be in a place where the family spends a lot of time. One of the worst things you can do to a puppy is to isolate him. He'll be happiest, and easier to train, when he's part of the family.

Making Him Like It

Don't think of the crate as a cage, but as a den. Dogs like small, cozy places. The best way to interest your dog in the crate is to make him connect it with positive things, like food.

City Dogs

Most cities have laws about dog poop! If you walk your dog in a downtown area, there is probably a pooper-scooper law. This means that you'll have to pick up after your dog. Just bring along a plastic bag (or two of them double-bagged) so that you can put your hand inside, grab the poop, and then turn the bag inside-out to hold the poop. Drop the bag into the nearest garbage can.

Begin by feeding him in his crate. Watch him and wait until he's done, then let him out and take the food dish out, also. (You don't want to leave food and water in the crate because it will get dumped over, and because you want to control his feeding schedule.) When he goes inside, say "Bed," so that he learns the command. Ideally, you want to be able to say "Bed" and have him go inside with no treat and no gentle nudge from behind.

Until he gets used to it, every time you want him to go in, toss a biscuit or other puppy treat into the crate. Gently close the door after he goes in, and tell him what a good dog he is.

At first, wait a few minutes and then let him out. You can also put him in the crate for a short amount of time with a special favorite toy that you save for crate time.

Each time you put him in the crate, leave him in there a few minutes longer. You're trying to make him think happy thoughts about the crate! You

Weird Dog Fact
Two million tons of dog poop are left on America's streets every year.

You can use treats during housetraining, to reward your dog each time he "goes" outside! Researchers have found that dogs learn faster when food treats are used to reinforce training.

Poop Happens

When the puppy has an accident—and he will—the important thing is to catch him in the act. Say "NO!" and pick him up, and take him outside to the potty spot.

Only correct your pup if you catch him in the act. This is very important. If you don't see him making the mess, don't correct him later. He won't make the connection between having pooped a while ago and your being mad later on when you find it. He may seem to act "guilty" if you find an accident, but his reaction is really nothing more than fear and anxiety because he can sense you're upset—though he doesn't quite understand why.

But do clean up the mess well with a product made for pet accidents. You don't want him to go back to that spot because it smells like a potty spot.

don't want him to think that every time he goes in, you're going to leave him for hours.

At some point, you will put him in the crate and walk away. He may cry at first, but it's important that he gets used to it. If he doesn't get properly housebroken, your parents may not want him in the house at all. That would be much worse for him.

It's a little like babies and car seats. It doesn't take long before a baby gets used to being in a car seat and finds it comforting to be safely strapped in.

Until the dog is housebroken, it's a good idea to keep him on a leash while you're in the house with him and he's out of the crate. You can tie the leash to your belt loop to make sure he doesn't wander off. That way, if he starts to pee or chew on a chair leg, you can correct the behavior right away. And he'll be happy to be doing things with you!

The Next Step

Feed your dog the same food on a regular schedule so that he does his other "business" on schedule, too. When his system is regular, he'll be easier to train.

Know what your dog needs. Puppies may need to go out every half-hour or hour, while older dogs need to go out just three or four times a day. Try to figure out when your dog wants to go out. Is it after a nap? After eating? Pay attention to the puppy's behavior.

Remember, don't wait until it's too late! Here are some of the times when he'll almost certainly have to "go":

May I go?

- first thing in the morning

- any time he wakes up from sleeping

- after eating

- after—or during!—playtime

You want him to go out often enough that he doesn't have accidents in the house. It's important to catch him before

Nighttime Crying

If you have a young puppy 8 or 9 weeks old, you may need to take him out once in the middle of the night. Make it all business—take him to the potty spot, give the command, give him a treat, and promptly return him to the crate for the rest of the night.

Older puppies need to be checked on if they cry at night, but be careful not to reward the crying. You don't, for example, want to play with the puppy or give him a treat in the hopes that he'll stop crying. That will just make him repeat the behavior the next night.

If puppies older than 10 or 11 weeks need to go out in the middle of the night, try taking away their water bowls at about 7 P.M. That will probably solve the problem.

he makes a mistake. Try a schedule like this at first: take the puppy out as soon as he wakes up in the morning, then right after eating, about 15 minutes after he drinks, after he wakes up from a nap, after he's had playtime, and right before bed.

Establish a potty spot, which is where you will bring your dog (on a leash) to "go." Always take the same route to the potty spot. When he goes, give a command like "Potty" or "Pee pee." Whether he pees or poops, call it the same thing. As soon as he goes, praise him and give him a treat. This may speed up your training. He will start to connect the act of "going" with the word you choose. Soon, you'll be able to take him somewhere, give the command, and he'll "go." This comes in very handy when you walk him in the pouring rain or freezing cold!

Dog Haiku

My master

is

home!

I am

thrilled,

delighted,

ecstatic!

And so

I piddle.

If you take him to the potty spot and he sniffs and wanders around without doing much of anything, take him back inside and put him in the crate. Wait 10 or 15 minutes and try again.

Paper Training

If you have a small dog, you can train her to go on paper inside rather than outside. (You need to choose either paper training or going outside, though. Doing both will be confusing.) You'll need a doggy exercise pen, about 4 feet by 4 feet. Set it up on a floor made of something that is easy to clean, like linoleum. Cover the floor inside the pen with newspapers. For about a week, keep the dog in the pen whenever you aren't watching her. Then, put a cushion or folded blanket in the pen for a bed and lay down just one newspaper (about 5 or 6 sheets thick). If she uses the paper the way she's supposed to, you can open up one end of the pen in a small area. Little by little, allow her to move all over the house when you are watching her. Tie her to you with a leash if you have trouble keeping track of her outside the pen. If she starts to go somewhere else, bring her right over to the papers. Go back to the beginning and try again if the problems continue.

Done!

How will you know your puppy is really housebroken? You can call your puppy housebroken if he rarely has accidents in the house, if he pees or poops outside when you give the command, and when you recognize his signals that he needs to go out, like barking or standing near the door. Congratulations!

Ring Bell for Assistance

Wouldn't it be handy if your puppy could tell you exactly when he had to "go"? After all, it's not always easy to figure out his need-to-pee signals.

Try this: On the door that you normally use to take your dog in and out, hang a bell (or string of bells) on the doorknob. Every time you take your pup outside, ring the bell before you open the door. Soon, the little guy will link the sound of the bell ringing with the door opening and will try to ring the bell himself, hoping the door will open! When this happens, praise him and take him on the leash to his potty area (this way he won't ring the bell just to go outside and play). Make sure he can't get to the bell when you aren't home because he'd get confused.

Oops!

Even after your dog's been housebroken, he may have times when he seems to forget what he learned. A number of things might upset him enough to cause him to backslide. He may be eating different food, a change in the weather might upset him, he might be sick, or he might be confused if he is at someone else's house. Be patient, be consistent, and you'll get him back on track.

What We Can Learn From Our Dogs

Don't just stroll, romp!

Leap!

Pounce!

Never turn down the chance to take a walk.

Protect your loved ones.

Take a **nap** whenever **you** feel like it.

Growl!

Just don't need to bite. Just

Most of the time, you don't need to bite. Just growl.

If you think something's there, **dig** until you find it.

Be delighted to see your family members when they come home.

Eat your dinner with gusto.

Love everyone, all the time, no matter what.

Figure out your place in the pack.

Forgive easily.

If you're a beagle, don't waste time wishing you were an English setter.

Expect to be patted.

Chapter 5

Grooming I know what you're thinking. Grooming is a little, uh, girly. Not at all! It has much less to do with looks and much more to do with the health of your dog. When you brush and bathe him, you can check for fleas, rashes and infections. You keep his coat shiny and brush out tangles and mats that can be uncomfortable. The specific kind of grooming your dog needs depends on his breed.

Brushing

Ask at a grooming salon what type of brush you should have for your dog. It will depend on the kind of coat he has, and whether or not he's still a puppy. (Puppies have more sensitive skin.) You'll find it easiest to have your pup on a leash when you groom him. When you brush him, work from his head to his tail and his shoulders to his paws. Don't forget his chest, belly, and tail. Brush in long, gentle strokes, and praise him when he stands still and cooperates.

Brushing Guidelines

Long-haired breeds: Brush daily

Medium-haired breeds: Brush weekly

Short-haired breeds: Brush monthly

If you find a mat or a tangle, start at the end and use a wide-tooth comb to work through it. Give him treats when you are done. Make it as much fun as a brushing can be so he doesn't fight you the next time.

My Dog Story

"When I brush Tashi, I put a little peanut butter in her Kong® toy so that she's distracted. She will get used to getting brushed pretty soon (just like my other dog did), and then I won't need the peanut butter trick."

—Thomas

Before your puppy's first bath, play games in and near the tub so that she associates it with something pleasant. Put treats on the side of the tub for her to find.

Next, place her in the tub with some toys and treats (but no water).

When she's comfortable playing in the tub, you can run the water and let it drain out.

When she's fine with the running water, allow it to fill the tub one or two inches.

Soon your dog will be fine with a regular bath!

Your dog likes taking about a bath about as much as you do—maybe less! But like you, he needs one now and then so that his coat stays clean. (You don't need to give him a bath more than once a month—maybe once every two or three months, or even less often. It just depends on how dirty he gets.)

Help your mom or dad look for a dog shampoo that is right for his age, coat, and skin. (The label should tell you.) Your parents can ask your vet or a dog groomer for advice if you're not sure.

The best place to bathe your dog is in a tub, with a rubber mat for him to stand on. You'll want to have his dog towel handy.

• Brush him first to get rid of extra hair.

• Put cotton balls in his ears to keep the water out.

• Wet him down with warm (not hot) water.

• Put a dollop of shampoo on the back of his neck and work it in, moving toward the tail.

• Gently work the shampoo into his coat, including underneath

Fleas?

Your dog has fleas if you can see "flea dirt," which looks like someone sprinkled pepper on your dog's skin. To figure out if what you are seeing is flea dirt, dampen a paper towel and rub the area; if the paper towel picks up a dark red color (blood), your dog has fleas.

In that case, have your parents talk to the veterinarian about the best and safest treatments. Your parents can also look into home remedies using things like lavender or cedarwood oils, vinegar, or peppermint.

Preventing fleas and ticks from getting on your dog is your best bet. You don't want to have to spend a weekend cleaning the house to get rid of fleas. Have your mom or dad ask the vet about products like Advantage and Frontline, which are drops applied once a month to the dog's skin. It's a bit expensive, but it's better for him than flea collars or flea powder. Your family can also try using special shampoos. Thera-Neem Pet Shampoo, for example, is organic and uses a special oil to repel fleas and chamomile to soothe inflamed skin.

and out to the tip of his tail.

• To wash his head, wet it first, then put a dab of shampoo on your hands and gently and carefully wash his face. Be sure to avoid his eyes. Tip his head back when you rinse his face.

• Rinse him well.

• If you are using the bathtub, pull the curtain closed and let him shake off.

• Rub him with a towel to help him dry off. Don't forget to thoroughly dry his legs, feet, and underside.

• You can carefully use a blow dryer and brush to finish the job if you want to. But always make sure the dryer is set on low, and don't hold it in one spot too long or get it too close to his skin.

The Other Stuff

Your dog's nails will have to be clipped, but this is best left to an adult, and probably a professional groomer. If you clip off more than just the ends and cut to the quick, it hurts and bleeds, and your dog will not be a happy pup. Also, many dogs don't like having their paws handled, so to get them to stay still while you trim can be tough. If you feel strongly about doing this yourself, have a professional groomer or your veterinarian teach you how to do it. Once the dog has been hurt while having his nails trimmed, it will be hard to get him to cooperate for another clipping session.

My Dog Story

"My mom makes a weird lemon-juice concoction to keep the fleas off of our dog. She slices up five or six lemons, puts them in a pitcher, then pours just enough boiling water to cover them. The next day, she puts the liquid in a spray bottle and squirts if all over the dog. He doesn't have fleas, so maybe it works!"

—Zachary

If your dog's ears need cleaning, this can be done by your vet or groomer. If you want to do it at home, you'll need for your parents to help. It involves buying dog ear cleaning solution and cotton balls and following the directions carefully. You don't want to go inside his ears—just clean the part of his ear that you can see. Dogs with long, floppy ears need a more thorough cleaning than those with little, perky ones. You can gently wipe away the stuff that gathers in the corner of a dog's eyes with warm water and a soft cloth. If you do this daily, it will never get too bad.

For details about nail clipping and ear cleaning, check out *dogs.about.com* and read through the section on grooming. To watch a video on "How to clip a dog's nails" (and for other helpful dog info), log onto *www.expertvillage.com*.

Skunked!

If your dog meets up with a skunk, you'll need the help of your parents! One of them can make a bath for your dog out of these ingredients:

- a quart of hydrogen peroxide
- ¼ cup of baking soda
- a squirt of mild liquid soap

Note: It's very important to keep the mixture out of the dog's eyes!

Scrub the dog thoroughly with this mixture, then rinse him with lukewarm water. (Your mom or dad will need to use rubber gloves and boots to keep from smelling like skunk!)

You can also buy an all-natural product called Omega Zapp Skunk Odor Pet Shampoo by NuHemp Botanicals, which can be used near the dog's face if that's where he was sprayed.

"If Dogs Had Their Own Bumper Stickers ..."

Cat Poop
It's What's for Dinner

★ ★ ★ ★ ★ ★ ★ ★ ★
I can LICK your HONOR STUDENT
★ ★ ★ ★ ★ ★ ★ ★ ★

HONK if you love eating garbage

WWLD:
What Would Lassie Do?

BACK OFF!
I didn't say you could sniff my butt

I'd rather be chasing this car

Friends Don't Let Friends
Drink From the Toilet

I ♥ CATS
They taste yummy!

POOP HAPPENS

Chapter 6

Out and About If you have a new puppy, you'll be eager to take her lots of places. For you, it will be fun to show her off. For her, it's important to experience a wide variety of people, places, other animals, and activities.

You'll have to wait, though, until she's had all her shots. Usually this isn't until she's at least 12 weeks old. Before then, she's at risk of catching some very serious dog diseases.

Also, when she's very young, she'll tire easily. Young pups can't be expected to keep going all day. It's hard on them. They need to sleep a lot while they're growing.

But once she's old enough, she will need to get out and experience all kinds of different situations. This is called *socialization*. If she doesn't get enough socialization before adulthood, there are some things that she might never be able to get used to later. Puppyhood is sort of a limited "window" of time when a dog needs to learn a lot about the world. Having different experiences helps her brain develop and makes her more comfortable with change later in life.

So take her to the park, to the beach, to the pet store, or anyplace safe where she's likely to encounter new things. You want her to learn about bikes, lawn mowers, cars, stairs—anything she hasn't seen. She should also be introduced (always on her leash) to other dogs, cats, horses and a variety of creatures.

If you have some treats with you, that will help her think happy thoughts about all of the new things she's seeing. You also want her to practice "taking care of business" away from her regular potty spot, so that you can take her places when you need to. Try to give her three new experiences each week.

Be prepared for your first few outings. Your puppy might act crazy! It will get easier, but your pup could be so excited about all of the new sights and smells that she stops listening to you, jumps on people, pees on every corner … you get the picture! Don't get freaked out. Keep giving commands as you would at home. Say "no" if you need to, and praise her when she deserves it. Don't let her get away with bad behavior just because there are other people around! This means that you'll have to be more focused on her than on the people. If someone wants to pet her, feel free to say, "Sure, just wait until I calm her down. I don't want her to jump on you." Even if others think it's cute when she jumps and say they don't mind, you know how you want her to behave.

Some puppies don't act crazy at all when they leave home. Instead, they're scared. Your puppy might hide behind you or lie down and whimper. You'll want to pat her to make her feel better, but don't. Act like the cool and confident leader that you are. Gently use the commands you've been teaching her at home. When she starts to walk beside you, give her a treat. If you stay calm and happy, she will follow your lead.

At home, you can prepare her for situations she'll face

The Littlest Puppies

Although he's too young to take out into public, you can expose your tiny pup (8 to 12 weeks) to different things around the house to get him ready to step into the world.

First, invite a few friends over to play gently with him. Every positive encounter he has will make him think that people are great!

To get him used to walking on different surfaces, put a variety of things on the floor, like big pieces of cardboard or bubble wrap.

By letting him play with things that are safe but noisy (like an empty plastic milk jug), he'll be less likely to be startled and upset when he's older and he faces unfamiliar things.

out in the world. Groom her so she gets used to staying still while she is being handled. Act like the vet and check her eyes, ears, belly, and legs. Get her used to things she might find when she leaves the yard: curbs, grates, and steps, for example.

On the Leash

Before you take your pup out, attach the leash to him when he is at home and let him drag it around to get comfortable with it. Keep an eye on him! If the leash gets caught on something, he could choke.

Happiness is a warm puppy.

—**Charles Schulz**

Next, tie the leash to your belt loop and do your chores around the house, or whatever you need to do. Get the dog

If your pup is tempted to chase cars (or joggers or bicyclists), lead by example. Act scared of the car! Whimper like a puppy and quickly go to the side of the road. Keep her behind you as the car passes and if she looks at the car, say "NO!"

Dogs feel very strongly that they should always go with you in the car, in case the need should arise for them to bark violently at nothing right in your ear.

—Dave Barry

used to moving with you rather than fighting with you when he's on the leash. When you begin taking walks, you can have tiny treats in your hand that you use to keep him walking beside you rather than running ahead, pulling on the leash. If he pulls, stop, and don't continue until the leash is slack.

In the Car

In the car, the safest place for your pup is in a crate. If you can't put him in a crate, you'll want to buy a dog seat belt. Your local pet store should carry a variety of these, or you can order one online. Wait to feed him until after the car ride so that he doesn't get sick. (If he does get sick, try putting him in a different seat to see if he feels better when he has a different view or a smoother ride.)

Even though dogs love to stick their heads out of car windows, it's not a safe thing for them to do, because pebbles or other things might fly into their eyes. If the window is open too much, the dog might even jump out if he sees a squirrel or something else enticing.

If your dog is afraid of the car or gets sick when he rides, try to get him used to the car gradually. Use it as a play space: In the driveway, open all the doors and let the pup jump in and out. Put treats or toys in the car for him to find. Ask your mom or dad to start the car, and let it run for a few minutes while you allow the dog to jump in and out and look for treats. Soon you can take a short trip to the end of the street and back. Little by little, your dog will start to think of the car as a fun place to be and won't be as nervous about taking a ride.

Weird Dog Fact
There are more than 400 million dogs in the world today.

Meeting Other Dogs

If you get together with a friend and his new puppy, expect things to start off with a bang! Dogs need to figure out who is "top dog," and this might involve a lot of growling, mouthing, jumping, and other bluffing behavior. This is especially true if the dogs are the same sex.

It helps if you introduce the dogs on neutral ground—that is, not your house or your friend's house,

where one of the dogs will feel like he's defending his turf.

At first, they should both be leashed. (If you are in a fenced-in area and things are going well, you can always drop the leash and let them play.) The getting-to-know-you bluffing will likely end with the dogs figuring out who is the dominant one, then settling in to play. Don't interfere unless they really start to fight, and even then just pull back on their leashes to separate them.

If you are out walking with your puppy and an unleashed dog approaches, be careful! Don't stop walking, don't look directly at the dog, and try not to let your puppy look at him. Walk away and keep the dog close to you on the leash. If you and your dog don't look threatening, an unleashed dog won't feel he needs to chase or attack you.

Meeting New People

The best way to teach your dog to like people is to make him associate

> **Weird Dog Fact**
> Labrador retrievers are the most popular dog breed in Boston, Chicago, and Los Angeles. In New York, poodles are number one, and in Miami, German shepherds take the top spot.

people with something good, like treats! If you keep his treats in a small container and always shake it just before you give him one, it won't be long before he'll hear the noise and think of treats. Then you can give the container of treats to anyone you want your dog to like, from the vet to your new neighbor. When the new person shakes the can, the dog comes, tail wagging, ready for a treat!

My Dog Story

"Last year I brought my dog to the park to meet up with a friend of mine and his dog. Unfortunately, the two dogs got into it. When we realized that it wasn't just dog play, we each took off our coats and threw them over our dogs' heads. It stopped them long enough for us to grab their leashes and separate them."

—Ben

DOGGY TIP

If you aren't able to separate two fighting dogs, try pouring or spraying water onto their heads. You may surprise them enough that they'll stop fighting, and you and your friend can grab their leashes and pull them apart. Carry a big water bottle with you so that you're prepared!

"Six Things You Thought You'd Never Do For Your Dog That You End Up Doing"

1. Talk baby talk to him.

2. Watch Animal Planet with him because it's his favorite channel.

3. Let him sit on your lap in the car so he can look out the window.

4. Carry him up and down the stairs when he decides that he's afraid of them.

5. Invite the new kid across the street over to play because your dog really likes his dog.

6. Put a bandana around his neck to make him look cool.

Chapter 7

Exercise Dogs need exercise, and exercise involves you! Exercise doesn't just keep your dog healthy, it also helps meet his social needs because he's interacting with you or with other dogs. But exercise doesn't have to mean taking him on the same walk three times a day. There are all sorts of ways to exercise your dog besides walking him.

You can get together with other friends who have dogs and let them play together, take a training class with your dog, or even ask your parents to take him to "doggie day care" if he's alone for long periods during the day. Check out Chapter 10 to read about all sorts of dog sports and activities.

There are some important things to know about exercising your dog. If you have a puppy who is less than four months old, you should play with him on a long leash rather than take him on an extended walk. His bones are still growing, and his tissues are soft and pliable. He's not ready for a five-mile hike yet!

Puppies aren't even ready for pavement, so keep yours on the grass or on dirt. Play actively with a little puppy about three times a day, for 10 minutes or so each time. Choose games that encourage good behavior. Instead of playing chasing games, for instance, toss a tennis ball or empty plastic bottle for him to fetch, or tie a toy to a string that is attached to the end of a stick and dangle the toy in front of the puppy. Before you take him on his first long walk, take short practice walks around the yard. After he's a year old, he is ready for more rigorous exercise.

The amount of exercise a grown dog needs depends on his size and breed. In general, big dogs need more exercise than little ones. Certain breeds, like Dalmatians, are very high-energy and need 20 or 30 minutes of exercise three times a day, while other breeds, like toy poodles or pugs, need just 5 or 10 minutes of exercise twice a day.

DOGGY TIP

To teach your dog to drop the ball after he fetches it, hold out a treat. He'll drop the ball to get the treat. Say "Drop" when he does so that he learns the command.

If you're going to be leaving your dog for a few hours, you'll want to give him exercise just before you go so he's more likely to sleep while you're gone. (A lot of dog trainers say that a good dog is a tired dog.) If your dog doesn't use up his energy with exercise, he may do destructive things like dig, bark, and chew.

To decide what kind of exercise your dog would like, think about his breed. For example, retrieving breeds like long games of fetch or swimming. No two dogs are alike, so you need to figure out what your dog likes to do best.

Be aware of the weather when you are exercising your dog. Since they can't sweat, dogs—especially those with thick coats—can overheat quickly when it's very hot outside. You're better off playing some games in the basement or waiting until evening, when it will be cooler.

Lazy Ways to Exercise Your Dog

Some days you just aren't up to getting yanked around the neighborhood by your dog on his leash. No prob—you can still make sure that your dog gets plenty of exercise! Try one or more of the no-sweat activities that follow:

Flashlight tag, doggy style. Go into the basement (or any dark area) and turn on a flashlight. Move the beam around the room, and watch your dog go crazy chasing the spot of light!

Fetch. The classic lazy ploy ... You throw the ball, the dog brings it back to you for more. If you have access to water and your dog is a great swimmer, you

can have him retrieve the ball from the water. (Bonus: It's the lazy way to bathe a dog!)

Toss a treat. Cut a hot dog into tiny pieces or grab a handful of small treats. Toss a treat into the grass so that your dog has to hunt for it. Once he finds it, toss another treat in the opposite direction so that he has to run and then hunt.

Back and forth. If you have a friend who is willing to help, this game will give your dog lots of exercise while also reinforcing the "come" command. Each of you should grab a handful of small treats and stand on opposite sides of the yard.

You begin by calling the dog: "Max, come!" Reward him when he comes. Then, your friend calls him and he runs to her. Continue doing this, with the dog running back and forth between you, until he is tuckered out!

Car chase. Rev up that remote-control car (the indestructible one!), and send it zipping down the hallway. Everyone knows that dogs love to chase cars, even tiny ones!

Tiny bubbles. Blow bubbles for your dog to chase. You'll get tired just watching him leap and pounce!

Roll Over and Play Dead

Come on, Max! Play dead! Play DEAD! DEAD, Max! You can do it Max! PLAY DEAD!

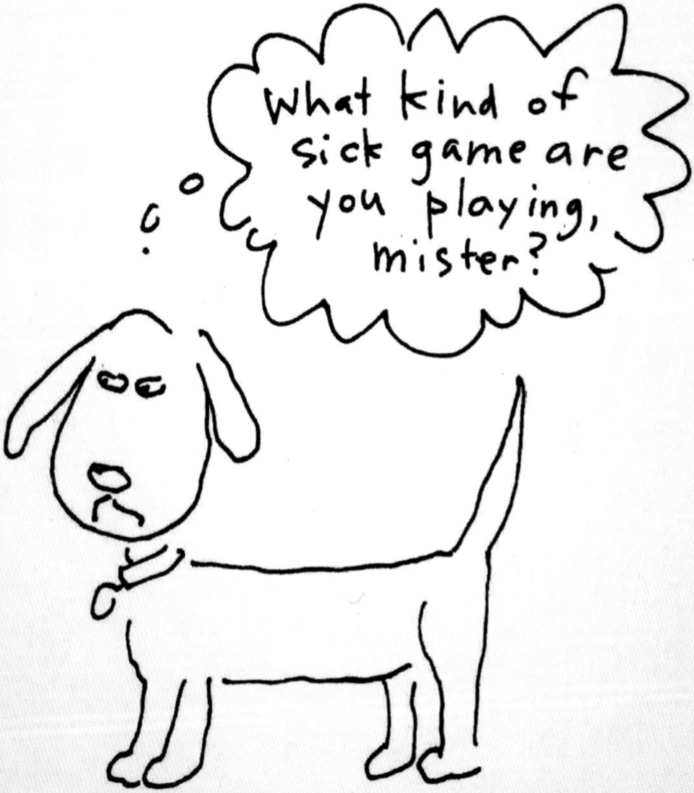
What kind of sick game are you playing, mister?

Chapter 8

Tricks, Treats, and Training You want your dog to be the cool, fun dog that everyone wants around, not the annoying dog that jumps on everyone or grabs food off of the dining room table. The first step is to teach him to behave himself so that he doesn't drive your friends (and your parents) crazy.

Decide with your parents what the household rules will be, and then stick together! Nothing confuses a dog more than you allowing him to sit next to you on the couch, then your dad scolding him an hour later for doing the same thing.

When he does something he's not supposed to, say a stern "No!" and give a quick tug on his leash (another reason to leave him on the leash when he's inside and still learning). Make it easy for him to be good by moving things that will tempt him, like chewable shoes (keep them in the closet) and trash baskets (scoot them under the sink).

The important thing to remember is that you don't want to reward bad behavior, like jumping up or begging for food. Here's the catch: What your dog thinks is a reward is different from what *you* think! If your dog grabs one of your mittens and you start chasing him and yelling at him to get it back, that's a reward for him! He got you to play with him! The trick is to ignore him when he's bad, if possible, and to reward him when he's good. When he's lying down quietly, that's the time to go pat him and give him a biscuit. When he's jumping up on you, fold your arms across your chest and look up. Don't reward him by giving him attention.

There is much more information on dog training than any one book

My Dog Story

"The more I got to know my dog Dusty, the easier it was to train him. At first, when he ran away from me, I chased him, which made him run more.

"Finally, I figured out that if I leaned down and pretended to have a treat in my hand, he would come out of curiosity to see what it was! So as long as I actually do have a treat sometimes, it works!"

—Justin

could cover. If you want more details on certain areas of dog training, visit *www.dogpatch.org*. From there, you can search for specific information or check out the forums where dog owners offer advice to one another.

Bad Dog!

If you have a dog that misbehaves, you'll need to correct his actions without hurting or hitting him. You can startle him by shaking an empty soda can that you've filled with pebbles or pennies (and taped shut with duct tape).

Some people set up booby traps for dogs that do things like jump onto furniture or get into the garbage. They might arrange for something very noisy to fall over that will startle the dog and discourage him from going back (like a pyramid of soda cans filled with pebbles or pennies and taped shut). Remember not to use anything that could be harmful to your dog, though.

The Four Commands Every Dog Should Know (and how to teach them)

A great way to start is to teach your dog these four commands: "come," "sit," "down," and "stay." When you train him, always use the same command word, and say it only once. Being consistent is very important in training your dog!

Use the dog's name before each command. Offer lots of treats and praise so that it's fun for him. Never punish him for getting it wrong. When you're done with a command (like sit or stay) say "Free!" in an excited way. That's known as a "release word." Then he knows he can move.

Come. This is probably the most important command to teach your dog. After all, if he's ever running toward a busy road, you'll want him to come when you call him!

Dog experts say that the most important thing about teaching "come" is to make sure that the dog doesn't think it means something bad will happen if he comes to you. If you tell him to "come" and then you scold him for digging or tie him up right away, he won't want to come the next time!

Doggone Funny
Q: What do you call a dog with no legs?
A: *It doesn't matter what you call him—he still won't come!*

The best way to teach this command is to reward him with a little treat and praise each time he comes. When you start to teach him, have him on a long leash in a small area. If he doesn't come the first time you call him, gently pull him toward you on the leash, and then praise him when he reaches you. Or you can step on his leash right away and keep him from moving.

Practice having him come from just a few feet away until he obeys. (If you have a friend who is willing to hold him while you step several feet away and call him, great!)

Sit. To teach this command, start by holding a treat just in front of your dog's nose. When he's looking at the treat, slowly bring it over his head so that his head comes up to follow it but his bottom goes down! As he begins to sit, say, "Sit!" (If he doesn't go into a sitting position naturally, you can gently help him tuck into that position.) When he is in a full sitting position, reward and praise him. Then release him with "Free!" Repeat this three or four times and then give him a break.

Stay. As soon as your dog knows "sit," it's time to teach "stay." Tell him to sit. With your open hand in front of his face, back one step away from him while saying, "Stay."

If he doesn't move, go back to him and reward him while he is still in the sitting/stay position. Try it again, but add a few more seconds each time. Then reward him after 10 seconds but keep him in a "stay"; reward him after another 15 seconds, and then free him.

Begin to take extra steps away from him as he learns to stay. If the dog follows you as you step back, say "no" and walk him back to the spot where he started. Give the "sit" command and try again.

Down. With the dog in a sitting position, lower a treat to the floor as he watches. He should follow the treat to the floor. If he doesn't, lift one front leg and gently press on the opposite shoulder.

Or, with the dog in a standing position, hold a treat in front of your dog, then move it down, between his front paws. As he begins to lower himself to get the treat, gently move your arm forward, pressing against his hind legs from behind

Continued on page 91

Tricks and Treats

If you want to do like the pros, have a little bag filled with treats that you attach to a belt loop. Try small treats that your dog can easily chew, like Cheerios® or tiny bits of hot dog or bologna. At the grocery store, you can buy "deli ends" for very little money. Surprise him with a different treat each time!

Guaranteed Way to Succeed at Dog Training

Teach Your Puppy Tricks He WANTS To Learn

"Jump over the fence! Good boy!"

"Come on, boy, bury the bone!"

"Sit on Papa's favorite chair! Jump up! Come on! Be a good boy!"

Top 8 Training Tips

1. Make sure everyone in the family uses the same commands so the dog doesn't get confused.

2. Even if it takes your dog a long time to come when you call him, reward him when he finally does. If you get angry when he comes because it took him too long, he'll learn not to come at all!

3. Make sure you take his bad behavior seriously. If you laugh because he jumps, or excuse it with "He's only a puppy," then you reinforce his bad habits.

4. Reward good behavior, but don't ever hit him when he's bad.

5. Reward him when he poops and pees outside, but don't push his face into an indoor poop. He won't understand what that means.

6. Only give a command if you are ready to follow through if he doesn't obey.

7. Be consistent!

8. Be patient!

to get him to go all the way down. In either case, give the "down" command as you are lowering the treat. (Holding your open hand over your head slightly in front of you while you say "down" is useful because then your dog will recognize the signal even if he can't hear you, like if he is on the other side of a busy street.)

What's "Clicker Training"?

Clickers are small, inexpensive gadgets that make a distinctive "click" sound. The idea behind clicker training is that, after a short training period, the dog will do what you tell him to when he hears the clicker.

To begin, give the dog a treat and immediately click. Do this 10 times. Repeat this several times a day for a few days. Then, every time the dog does something you want him to, you "click and treat," that is, you make the clicking sound and offer a treat. If he jumps on you, ignore him, then click and treat when he stops jumping. If he chews on one of his toys (instead of your baseball bat), click and treat.

Soon he will hear the clicking sound and be as excited about that as he is when he gets a treat. In his mind, the clicker means something good, so he will act in a way that will make his owner click! Some dog owners believe that it works just as well to say enthusiastically, "Good dog!" rather than click, and then offer a treat.

Teaching Tricks

Dogs spend a lot of time being bored. In years past they herded sheep, hunted or retrieved birds for dinner, and defended the land from predators. Today, they nap, they eat, and they chew on squeaky toys. So learning tricks is fun for your dog! She loves spending time with you, making you happy, and learning new things. And you'll love showing off how smart she is to your buddies. Once you've taught her the basic commands, it's time to teach her some fun tricks!

Ten Cool Movie Tricks to Teach Your Dog

It might seem like teaching a dog to dance or to crawl would be pretty hard. But there's a trick to training your dog to do unusual stunts: Simply reward the behavior and name it whenever the dog does it! Do you want your dog to sneeze on command? When the dog sneezes, give the command, "Sneeze!" and praise and reward her! If your dog rolls on his back in the grass, tell him to "Roll over!" and give him a treat and words of praise. This is sometimes called "capturing" a behavior.

"Shaping" a behavior is when you help the dog learn a trick. If you want him to ride in a little wagon, for instance, you reward him when he first goes up to the wagon, then reward him when he sniffs it, then reward him when he puts a paw on it. You may have to lift him into the wagon but reward him for staying there for a few seconds. If he stays in while you pull it a few inches, another treat!

Soon you will have shaped his behavior so that he knows that you want him to jump into the wagon and sit there while you pull him.

Break each trick into small steps. Also, make each training session short so he doesn't get tired. Puppies can pay attention for about 5 minutes at a time; adult dogs can focus for 20 minutes at a time. Repeat the training sessions throughout the day.

Play the piano. You'll need a small toy piano for this trick. Place it near the dog and when he sniffs it, reward him. Every time he sniffs at or paws the piano, give him a little treat. Then start rewarding him only when he hits a key, and finally only when the key makes a sound. Scratch gently under one foreleg and then the other to encourage him to lift his paws. Soon he'll be playing a tune (OK, a bad tune, but a tune!) for a treat and will be ready for a recital!

Dog School

You'll find dog classes more fun than algebra and Spanish. Why not try out a class with your pup just for fun? Your mom or dad can call your local humane society, your veterinarian, or a nearby dog breeder and ask for a recommendation. (Or they can ask for recommendations for a personal dog trainer, someone who works just with you and your dog.)

Achoo! Go get me a tissue! This is just a fancy game of fetch that you can teach your dog one step at a time! If your dog already knows how to fetch, just play with a tissue you've made into a ball.

Reward him each time he brings the tissue to you. Eventually, lay a less-crumpled tissue on the floor for him to fetch. When he brings it to you, say "Achoo!" and reward him. Move the tissue closer and closer to the tissue box and say "Achoo!" each time he brings a tissue to you. Finally, tuck it into the top of a tissue box. Make sure you "sneeze" and reward him each time he brings you a tissue.

Spin in a circle. With the dog standing in front of you, say "Circle" and encourage him to turn using a treat. When he has made a complete turn, give him the treat and praise him.

When he gets good at doing the trick this way, you'll want to be able to give him the command from a few feet away. Help him learn this by attaching the treat to a long dowel or pole.

Turn off the light. Find a light switch that the dog can reach when she's standing on her hind legs. Then hold a treat above the switch and say, "Lights out!" When the dog jumps up for the treat, she should hit the switch with her paw. (You can help by guiding her paw.)

Treat and praise her when the light goes out. As she gets better, move away from the switch and treat her when she jumps up and hits the switch.

Be bashful. Start with the dog in a down position. Holding a treat, say, "Hide eyes" as you lift his paw to his muzzle. You can even try blowing gently into his face to make him paw at his eyes. Any time the dog swipes at his face with his paw, say the command "Hide eyes!" and reward him.

Dinner time! Your dog will look like Snoopy if he masters this trick! Grab a lightweight dish that he can pick up easily, and toss it like a Frisbee® to prompt the dog to go and get it. Say "Bring your dish!" When he brings it to you, put a treat in the dish and praise him.

Repeat this several more times. Now put the dish down and say "Bring the dish!" If he needs encouragement, show the treat or shake the treat box.

Jump through a hoop. First, you'll have to teach the command "Jump!" Place a board or piece of sturdy cardboard in a doorway. With your dog on a leash, run toward the doorway and jump together over the board, giving the command as you do. If your dog hesitates, try a board that isn't as high. Treat and praise him on the other side of the board.

Once he's mastered that jump, replace the board with a Hula Hoop® that is held vertically on the floor. Keep him on

the leash and guide him through the hoop, praising him and giving him a treat when he goes through. As he gets used to the hoop, begin to raise it off the ground, a bit higher each time he goes through.

Soon he'll be able to jump through the hoop on command! (If you want him to make a grand entrance for his birthday party, hang paper streamers from the top of the hoop and have him burst through!)

S-P-E-L-L. As soon as your dog learns to sit on command, add a hand signal while saying "Sit." An example of a hand signal would be your hand held up in a fist. For several days, use both the command and the hand signal. Soon, the dog will respond to the hand signal without the command. As soon as he does, you can say, "S-I-T" while you give the signal and he will sit. The next step is to drop the hand signal and just spell the word. You can use the same technique with any command he already knows, like "Down," "Stay," or "Come." Your dog will look like he's ready for first grade!

Wave goodbye. Begin with your dog in the sit position. Facing her, wave your hand, and gently push her front paw up. When she lifts it, say "Bye bye." Hold her paw up for just a second or two. Let it drop, then give her a treat and praise. After some practice, she should raise her paw when you wave!

Take a bow. Because this trick involves naming and rewarding a common dog behavior, it's an easy one to teach! You just need to be able to react quickly and have treats at hand. When the dog stretches out with her butt in the air and her head down, say "Take a bow!" Then give her a treat while she's in the bowing position.

Weird dog fact

Have you ever heard people talk about Pavlov's dogs? Ivan Pavlov was the scientist who noticed that his dogs started drooling when they heard the footsteps of the person who always fed them! He learned that dogs can learn to link events that aren't normally connected. Footsteps wouldn't normally make a dog drool. But when the dogs figured out that certain footsteps meant that food was coming, they began drooling!

Have you noticed this with your dog? Does he start to jump around if you get your coat because he thinks you're taking him for a walk? (This is how clicker training works!)

Teaching an Old Dog New Tricks

It's not true what they say—you *can* teach an old dog new tricks! It may take a little longer and require more patience on your part, but it can be done. Most older dogs can learn anything that a puppy can, and the training techniques are very much the same.

One tip with an older dog is to use a super-duper treat as a reward rather than something he's used to. He'll want to do the trick again to get that amazing treat!

When your older dog does something naturally, name the behavior ("Good boy, SIT") and reward him with his irresistible reward. Next, just give the command once, and reward him if he responds. Don't give the command more than once, but do say it loudly if the dog is a little hard of hearing. If he doesn't do what you tell him, ignore him. Don't punish him and don't keep repeating the command. In a little while, you can try again.

Teach more complicated commands or tricks in stages, but use the same method. You can also change an older dog's behavior this way. If he barks too much, praise, treat, and name it when he's quiet ("Good boy, quiet!"). When he pees or poops where you want him to, reward him and name it.

The real reward for older dogs is that when they are involved in learning new things, they stay mentally alert and active for a longer time. Dogs love to be busy, and they love to please you. It is great for their mental and physical health if you are working to teach them new things.

Pup Quiz: Match the Dog with the TV Show

You may want to get other family members to help you with this quiz!

1. Brian
2. Eddie
3. Astro
4. Comet
5. Tiger
6. Mr. Peabody
7. Fred
8. Marshmallow
9. Ruff
10. Bandit

___The Brady Bunch
___The Adventures of Rocky and Bullwinkle
___Malcolm in the Middle
___I Love Lucy
___Frasier
___Full House
___Family Guy
___Dennis the Menace
___Little House on the Prairie
___The Jetsons

Answer key:
5. The Brady Bunch, 6. The Adventures of Rocky and Bullwinkle, 8. Malcolm in the Middle, 7. I Love Lucy, 2. Frasier, 4. Full House, 1. Family Guy, 9. Dennis the Menace, 10. Little House on the Prairie, 3. The Jetsons

Chapter 9

Understanding Your Dog Admit it: You've wished that you could talk to your dog, haven't you? Wouldn't it be great if you could ask your dog why he's always digging holes next to the fence or why he pulls your father's underpants out of the laundry basket and waves them around like a flag? Well, in many ways, it is possible to figure out what your dog thinks and to understand why he does the things he does.

Speaking Dog

Your dog has a lot to say, and he "talks" to you through his body movements as well as through his barks and other noises. If you want to understand him better, pay attention to his tail, ears, eyes, and mouth. You can learn to speak "dog"!

> Dogs are obsessed with being happy.
>
> —James Thurber

The way a dog positions and moves his tail tells you what he is thinking. Even though a dog's tail was originally meant to help him keep his balance, it has evolved to help him communicate with us and other living creatures.

For instance, a fast, wide sweeping of a dog's tail says that he's happy and excited; a slow wag can mean he's confused. When a dog's tail is horizontal, sometimes it means that the dog is going to challenge another creature. The tail of a confident dog is up and over the dog's back, while a frightened dog keeps his tail down, between his legs.

Weird Dog Fact About a third of dog owners talk to their dogs on the phone.

A wagging tail doesn't always mean a dog is friendly. If a dog's tail is high and stiff as it quickly wags, that is one dog that should be left alone!

A dog's other body parts "talk," too. When his ears are up, he's paying attention and interested in what's happening around him. When they're down, he's afraid or unsure. Another sign that a dog is a bit anxious is when he yawns or gives his nose a quick lick. When a dog tilts his head, he's a little confused, and may be trying to hear better so he can understand.

A raised paw doesn't mean he wants to shake your hand! He's telling you that he understands that you're in charge. When a dog puts his paws and elbows on the ground with his butt in the air, which is known as a "play bow," he is saying that he wants to have fun! He sends the same message when he brings a toy to you and drops it at your feet or when he jumps and runs and dances around.

Dogs also use different barks to get their messages across. The meaning comes from the pitch and tone of each bark. Scientists from Hungary actually developed a computer program that they say can translate a dog's barks into words like "stranger," "fight," "walk," "alone," "ball," and "play."

The number-one way life would be different if dogs ran the world: All motorists must drive with their heads out the windows.

— **David Letterman**

Here's how you can learn to understand your dog:

High, long bark or yapping: Your dog is upset or lonely and needs your comfort.

Several quick barks: Your dog wants to play!

Solo bark: Your dog is just checkin' in.

Sharp and urgent or low barks: Your dog is protecting you.

Howling: Your dog wants to chat with other dogs. He is lonely and wants to bring the pack together.

Growling: Your dog is telling you that he is upset and might bite.

Yelp: Your dog is hurt or afraid. Help!

Answers to Your Best Dog Questions

Does my dog have a sense of humor?

Even though your dog makes you laugh sometimes, he probably doesn't intend to. It may seem like he does because he repeats the things you laugh at, but that's because you rewarded him with positive attention. On the other hand, dogs are able to tease, like when they run to you with a ball and then veer away at the last minute so that you can't get it.

Pup Quiz
The Basenji is the only dog that can't:
a. wag his tail
b. bark
c. hear

Answer: b (But a Basenji does yodel—really!)

Dog Haiku

Every day
the
bad
postman
comes.

I bark and
bark,

he goes away.

I'm scary.

If teasing is a type of humor, then it could be said that dogs have a sense of humor.

Does my dog dream?

Many scientists believe that all mammals dream, including dogs. During sleep, the brain sorts through things that happened during the day. When your dog twitches and yelps, he is remembering his day. We don't know if dogs have imaginations, though, which is where humans get a lot of the ideas for our dreams.

Does my dog love me as much as I love him?

The big question is, what the heck is "love"? After all, people who claim to be in love often break up and leave one another, and sometimes end up hating each other! You don't hear about dogs that suddenly unlove their owners and run away. Love is complicated!

Many dog experts believe that dogs do feel "dog love" for their owners. Sure, they may love their owners in part because they receive food, water, and shelter from them—perhaps children love their parents for many of the same reasons!

Dogs can be quirky, and that can be fun, but some dog behavior is not acceptable. Your parents might need to seek expert help from your vet or a dog trainer if your dog exhibits aggression (like biting or growling) or obsessive-compulsive behavior (like constantly eating socks or digging).

They should also call in a professional if your dog regularly pees in the house when nervous or excited, or is very destructive when left alone.

Dogs can certainly become extremely attached to their owners. Until we speak the same language, though, we may never know exactly how our dogs feel.

Dog Haiku

Lick

myself,

lick the trash

can lid;

now

I run over

to lick

your face.

Does my dog feel guilty when he does something wrong?

No, guilt is a human emotion. If a dog thinks his owner is angry, though, he will act in a submissive way. He might hang his head down or tuck his tail under. This is because in a wolf pack, a wolf would act like this to avoid a fight with a dominant wolf. Dogs and wolves have a great deal in common. Scientists believe that dogs evolved from wolves that were tamed by humans about 15,000 years ago.

When your dog acts "guilty," he actually doesn't know what you are angry about but is sensing your emotion and is feeling fearful and anxious. It may seem that he's "acting guilty," but his behavior is simply his way of signaling that he wants to avoid a fight with you, just as he'd do with another animal in his pack.

Does my dog understand me?

Dogs may recognize a number of words, especially words that mean something to them, like "walk," "vet," or "dinner." They understand that certain words like "eat" are followed by food, so they make a point of noting that!

The tone of our voice matters even more than the words we use. If you don't believe this, say the same nonsense word happily, and then sternly. See if your dog reacts the same way to both.

There are a lot of misunderstandings between a dog and his

boy, though. If your dog is begging at the table, for instance, and you give him food to make him stop, he thinks he's being rewarded for begging and he'll do it even more! If he poops in the house, and you find it, and then start yelling at him, he thinks, "Hmm … next time I'd better find another place to poop, like behind the sofa or in the closet!"

> Dogs read the world through their noses, and write their history in urine.
>
> —J. R. Ackerley

So even though you may feel that you and your dog understand each other, there may be times when people-speak doesn't quite translate.

Does my dog have a sixth sense?

Some people think that dogs have ESP (extrasensory perception) or other special powers. Most experts are skeptical about that, but they do point out the reasons people might believe that to be true.

Dogs have very sensitive hearing, so they pick up on things (like a tree starting to fall or a car coming down the road) before we do. When they react to things before we even know something is happening, we might think they can see into the future, when in fact they're just able to hear sounds we cannot.

Sometimes we notice specific things our dogs do that make them seem particularly smart. If your dog is waiting for you at the window when you come home from school, you might think he has the special ability to sense when you are coming home. But he might have looked out the window 30 other times when you weren't coming up the driveway—it's just that no one noticed those times!

It's safe to say that while dogs can't see into the future or read minds, they do have some highly developed senses that pick up on things before humans do.

Pup Quiz

In the "dogs don't always make great choices" category, here is a list of things that you might think are impossible for a dog to eat. Put a check beside each item on the list that you think a dog owner has reported as an accidental dog "meal."

___entire tub of margarine

___stack of prom photos

___exchange student's passport

___car keys, with keychain

___3 quarters and a dime

___wallet

___cactus

___squirrel

___bag of frozen peas

___bar of modeling clay

___firewood

___used Kleenex

___VCR remote control

___wicker basket

___disposable razor

___straight pins

___golf balls

___rocks

___4 boxes of chocolate-covered cherries

___steel shavings

___ball bearings

___cat poop

___mini-blinds

___library book

___lit fireworks

___paycheck

___lottery tickets

___fish hooks

___underpants

___panty hose

Answer: Dog owners have reported every item on this list to veterinarians or poison control hotlines. Yikes!

Why does my dog do that?

In some ways, dogs are so much like fuzzy little people. They love to cuddle, they can't wait to run outside and play games, they cry when they're upset.

But in other ways, their behavior is not at all like ours. It's hard to understand why a dog would ignore the delicious hamburger we made for him and instead try to swallow a dirty sock. Or why a dog would rather chew on the corners of the kitchen cabinets than chew on the cool $15 plastic squeaky hot dog you just bought her at the pet store.

Dog experts have come up with some likely reasons dogs do the things they do:

Why does my dog drink out of the toilet?

Why not? He doesn't understand what we use a toilet for, but he does know that a toilet is always full of cold water and it won't tip over. And on hot days, a tile bathroom floor feels great on the pads of his feet!

> I wonder what goes through his mind when he sees us peeing in his water bowl.
>
> —Penny Ward Moser

Why does my dog eat grass?

Dogs may eat grass because it provides certain vitamins they don't get in their food. Some people believe that dogs eat grass if they have an upset stomach, to make themselves throw up whatever is bothering them. Not even scientists who study dogs are sure about this one!

Why does my dog jump up on me?

There are two possible answers to this question. Some experts say that a dog jumps up to establish dominance. Maybe he wants to let you know he's top dog by getting as tall as he can!

But the most likely explanation is that it's part of friendly face-to-face communication, and that the dog simply is happy and excited and wants to get closer to you.

DOGGY TIP

You might be able to discourage jumping up by ignoring your dog. If that doesn't work, try walking into him so that he's forced down, telling him to "Sit," and then praising him for doing so. You can also step on his leash just as he's starting to jump up.

> Dogs need to sniff the ground; it's how they keep abreast of current events. The ground is a giant dog newspaper, containing all kinds of late-breaking dog news items, which, if they are especially urgent, are often continued in the next yard.
>
> **—Dave Barry**

Why does my dog smell other animals' butts?

A dog gets lots of information by smelling another dog's butt: whether the dog is male or female, what she likes to eat, her age, and whether she is ready for mating. Chemicals called pheromones that come from a dog's behind tell one dog about another. When two dogs approach one another, the dominant dog sniffs the other one first.

Why does my dog roll in horse manure, mud, or anything that smells bad?

A dog's sense of smell helps him to communicate with the world. Rolling in something he finds tells the world about his discovery! Or maybe, to your dog, the smell of deer poop is great! It's like putting on perfume! This behavior could also be due to a dog's interest in camouflaging his smell. That would have helped wild dogs long ago by covering their own scent with other smells, so they could go hunting without being detected.

Why does my dog love to put her head out of the car window?

Dogs stick their noses out of the window for the same reason your parents read the newspaper: to

> Did you ever notice that when you blow in a dog's face he gets mad at you, but when you take him in a car he sticks his head out the window?
>
> **—Steve Bluestone**

Weird Dog Fact

"Superlative" Dogs

The fastest dog: Greyhound
The tallest dog: Irish Wolfhound
The smallest dog: Chihuahua
The heaviest dog: Saint Bernard

find out what's going on in the world. Because they have many more smell receptors than we do, they get most of their information through their noses. Some dog experts say that a dog nose is 40 or more times more sensitive than a human nose! A dog can smell one drop of blood in five quarts of water! (For safety's sake, it's best to crack the window rather than let your dog stick his entire head out.)

Why does my dog chew shoes?

Puppies chew because their teeth are coming in, and chewing makes their gums feel better. At this stage, they have a very strong need to chew on something. Shoes are nice and soft, and available, because they're right on the floor! They also have interesting smells—from you and from all of the places you've been walking!

Older dogs chew if they are bored or worried because it calms them down. Shoe leather, in particular, tastes good to them and is fun to chew.

DOGGY TIP

Take a shoe-chewer to your local pet store and let her pick out several toys that she can gnaw on.

Try putting a dab of peanut butter on one or two toys before you give them to her.

Why does my dog walk around in a circle before lying down?

This behavior is left over from when dogs were wild. They needed to pat the grass down to create a comfy nest and establish their own area. Some researchers think that dogs made an extra large bedding area so that when predators came sniffing around, they would think that the dogs were a whole lot bigger than they really were and decide not to stick around!

Why does my dog like to dig?

She might be bored, need exercise, or be super high-energy. Or she might dig to make a cooling or heating pit, or to bury food for later. There's also the chance that she might just enjoy the fun, different smells that waft up from a newly dug hole! Some dogs, like terriers, were bred to dig because they found foxes and badgers by digging—it's in their blood!

DOGGY TIP

If your dog likes to dig, why not get him a children's sandbox? Bury cool, gross-smelling things or dog treats that he'd love to dig up! Often this will satisfy a diehard digger's urges.

Meanwhile, fill his favorite digging holes with dog poop. He'll be less likely to go back to the old spots!

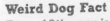

Weird Dog Fact

Every 12th year is the year of the dog, according to the Chinese. This means that people born in those years (1982, 1994, 2006 ...) have personalities like dogs: loyal, honest, friendly, and protective.

Why does my dog lick me?

Puppies know to lick their mother's faces in search of food, so it's a natural behavior. Your dog licks you to get your attention and your approval. He is telling you that he understands you're his "parent" and the top dog! It is a sign of affection and respect. Some dogs, like golden retrievers, are more likely to lick than others.

Why does my dog bark when the mail carrier comes?

Your dog thinks he's protecting you when he barks at someone who comes into your yard. And just think: his barking works! He barks at the person delivering the mail, and then that person leaves. Your dog thinks that he chased him away by barking!

Why does my dog chase cats?

Dogs instinctively like to chase, and cats just happen to be handy. Because wild dogs were hunters, some of that behavior is

Weird Dog Fact

Dogs pee against trees, buildings, and lampposts so that their "marks" are at nose level for the next dog that comes sniffing along. Dogs "mark" to say, "This is MY turf!" Dogs especially enjoy peeing on top of another dog's mark. It would be like putting up a student council election poster at school on top of a poster for the kid who's running against you!

Continued on page 114

Dusty checks pee-mail

My Dog Story

"My dog used to do some pretty bad stuff if we left him alone for too long. We finally figured out a few things we could do to keep him from digging, barking, and other things. We always took him for a long walk before we left so he was tired. We also left him with something to do. His favorite thing is when we put his dry dog food into an activity ball so that he has to work to get his food."

—Nick

still evident. When something runs, they give chase!

Some dogs understand that the family's cat should not be chased but will chase other cats outside. If a cat stands and fights back, however, many dogs will back off.

Weird dog fact

There is actually a word for when a dog eats out of a cat's litter box: coprophagy. *It seems pretty gross to humans, but for dogs, it may be a way to get certain vitamins, or it may be that the cat's poop tastes enough like the cat's food to be kind of yummy. After all, dogs only have 2,000 or so taste buds (people have about 9,000), so they aren't exactly going to appreciate fine dining!*

You don't have to worry about this behavior unless it becomes excessive. If so, have your parents talk to your dog's vet.

Why do dogs have black lips?

Long ago, dark skin protected dogs from the sun, so that dogs have dark noses, and dark around their eyes, and around their mouths. In recent times, dogs have certain features because of selective breeding. People decide that they think a certain thing is attractive, and so they breed more of the dogs with that feature, like black lips!

Why does my dog freak out at thunder?

No one really knows what part of thunder scares dogs—the lightning flashes, the thunder booms, or the sound of the wind and rain. Certain breeds, like collies, German shepherds and hounds, are more likely to be upset by storms. Dogs that come from shelters also tend to be more fearful of storms, maybe because they were abused in the past.

Although some dogs can adapt to loud noises like the sound of thunder, others can have a permanent, nearly incurable phobia of storms. Have your mom or dad talk to your vet if your dog seems to be seriously traumatized every time a storm rolls through.

Six Uses for a Dog You Might Not Have Thought of

paper shredder

Shovel

alarm clock

foot stool

door bell

personal trainer

Chapter 10

Fun and Games With Your Dog The whole idea behind owning a dog is having fun with him! There are all sorts of ways to have fun together, from a simple game of fetch to competitive events and daring adventures. Try a few different games to find the best way for you to play with your pet!

Games You Can Play With Your Dog

Playing games is what dogs do best! Invent your own, or try one of these.

Hide and Seek

Tell your dog to sit and stay, or have someone hold him, while you find a place to hide. When you're ready, call him and see if he can find you! (He may need you to call him a few times if he's stumped.)

Find the Treat

Tell your dog to sit and stay, or have someone hold her. Hide several strong-smelling treats where she can get to them without too much trouble. (You can play this game outside, too, by hiding treats behind trees or rocks, or by pushing them an inch or so into the snow!) Free her and see if she can find all of the treats!

If she has trouble with this, begin by having her smell the treat, then let her watch while you put it down, then free her to get it. Move the treat farther and farther away each time until it's out of sight.

Which Hand?

Put a treat in one hand and close your fists. Offer both fists to your dog. Did she go to the one with the treat? If she did, reward her! If not, just ignore her until she gets it right.

Hansel and Gretel

Make a trail using pieces of treats. At the end of the trail, put a special treat, like a piece of bologna. As your dog gets better at this game, place the treats farther and farther apart.

Follow Me

Tie a toy to the loop end of a short leash, and clip the other end around your ankle. Now move around as you normally would, doing chores or playing games, and your pup will follow you (or at least he'll follow the toy!).

Grand Slam

Hit tennis balls with a racquet and have your dog bring them back to you.

Swing low

Tie an empty plastic bottle to the end of a long rope and swing it around like a cowboy with a lasso so that the dog chases it.

Games You and Your Friends Can Play With Your Dog

If your friends come over and want to play with you and your new dog, here are some fun games to try.

Bounce 'n' Guess

To start, each of you picks a number between one and five. Then, on a hard floor, bounce a tennis ball to your pooch. Count the number of bounces the ball makes before he catches it. Whoever guessed right, wins!

Come to ME!

Here's another fun game to play with your dog and your buddies that also reinforces the command "Come." Stand around him in a circle. Take turns saying, "Come!" If he comes, give him a treat. Is there anyone he won't go to? Or someone he really likes? How many times in a row will he come?

Milk Jug Keep-Away

Find a few empty plastic milk bottles, and have a pair of your friends stand about 30 feet away from you and another buddy. (This is best as an outdoor game in a fenced-in yard.) Your dog can be in the middle.

Begin by kicking the milk jugs back and forth from one pair to the other. The dog will try to grab them as they are heading across the yard. Don't chase him for it; play with a different one until he brings back the one he grabbed. (You can also roll Frisbee® discs to each other and see if the dog can intercept one!)

Mind Games Your Dog Likes to Play with You!

So you think you know all of your dog's favorite games? Not so! Your dog has his own special games that he likes to play with you, whether you want to play or not! Maybe your dog has played one of these games with you.

Throw Up Something No One Can Identify

How it's played: The dog waits under the table until the family is gathered for dinner. The dog then hacks and chokes for several minutes, finally throwing up something no one can identify. The dog sits back and enjoys listening to people accuse one another of feeding him something that made him sick. (He knows that it was the squirrel head he ate, but he will never admit it.) He waits with glee to see who will be named as the guilty one, knowing that person will be stuck with cleanup duty.

Pretend to Forget the Trick

How it's played: The boy teaches his dog to roll over and play dead. The dog performs the trick perfectly 10 times in a row, to the delight of the boy. The boy invites all of his friends over to play video games—and to show off his smart dog.

When everyone arrives, he tells the dog to roll over and play dead. The dog stares blankly at the boy. The frustrated boy repeats the command. The dog pounces over to the TV and begins chewing on one of the controllers. The dog is sent to the basement for the rest of the afternoon.

When his friends are gone, the boy brings the dog back upstairs, at which time the dog rolls over and plays dead perfectly, 10 times in a row.

Shake Off!

How it's played: The dog has a bath, goes for a swim, frolics in the rain, or otherwise gets soaking wet. The boy tries to dry the dog off with a towel, but the dog doesn't like that idea and dances into the house, where he searches for the youngest and oldest members of the family. He waits until they are near one another, and then shakes vigorously, spraying water over both. The youngest one cries, the oldest one shrieks, and the dog is happy.

The game ends when the dog jumps on the couch and finishes drying off on an expensive antique quilt.

Pet Projects: Easy Dog Toys to Find and Make

Making dog toys is as easy as rummaging around in the garage or the recycling bin! You just need to make sure that the toys will hold up to a lot of biting and chewing, with no pieces that could cut your pup or be swallowed. Here are some quick and easy toys to find or make for your number-one pet.

- two tennis balls stuffed into an old sock, with knots at the cuffs and between the balls

- a bucket filled with water and with meatballs floating in it (bobbing for meatballs!)

- a treat tucked inside an old sock

- a cardboard paper-towel tube wrapped in duct tape

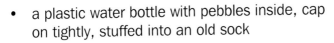

- a plastic water bottle with pebbles inside, cap on tightly, stuffed into an old sock

- strips of an old towel, braided to form a "tug"

- the leg of an old pair of jeans, tied with knots

- a piece of old garden hose or rope

- an empty plastic milk jug with a handful of dry dog food inside

- marrow bones that the dog has already chewed, with peanut butter smeared in both ends

- a big, plastic bouncy ball that you've outgrown

- a partly deflated soccer ball that he can grab in his mouth

- a tennis ball with a penny-sized hole (ask a parent to do the cutting) and treats stuffed inside

It's cold and rainy outside. You've already watched two hours of *Lassie* reruns together, and a half-hour of Animal Planet. You and your pup are bored. Now what?

How about setting up an obstacle course in your house? (This is best for small and medium-sized dogs.) Make tunnels and hurdles from empty boxes, footstools, and a yardstick propped at the right height. Use your imagination!

Hurdles are best on carpet (so the dog doesn't slip) and in a hallway (because the dog will have to go over, not around them).

Toilet plungers make great posts to weave around like a slalom skier. (Set them up about 2 feet apart.)

Make a doggie balance beam from a bench or a rolled-up carpet.

Run next to him so he knows what you want him to do. Hold a Hula Hoop so that the dog can jump through it, and lure him with a treat.

When your dog does what he's supposed to, say the command "Jump!" or "Up!" or "Over!" Use treats to lure him into a tunnel or over a hurdle.

If you have a friend with a dog, invite him over and you can have an obstacle-course race!

Doggone Funny
Q: What do you get if you cross a dog with a frog?
A: *A dog that can lick you from across the street!*

Dogs laugh, but they laugh with their tails.

—**Max Eastman**

According to a *Washingtonian* magazine survey, almost 40 percent of dog owners said that their dogs like to watch TV! Here is a list of the best movies to watch at home with your pooch.

101 Dalmatians – In this animated Disney classic, nasty Cruella De Vil steals a litter of 15 Dalmatian puppies from Pongo and Perdita (and then grabs 86 more puppies) so that she can make a fur coat out of them. The canine parents are determined to rescue all of the puppies.

Benji – Shot from a dog's-eye view, this movie follows Benji from homeless mutt to canine hero. The smart and capable pooch manages to rescue the kidnapped children of the family who adopted him.

Lady and the Tramp – This animated film from Disney features the relationship between the pampered purebred Lady and the street-smart mutt Tramp. Despite misadventures and misunderstandings, there's a happy ending.

All Dogs Go to Heaven – In this film set in New Orleans in the 1930s, a rough German shepherd named Charlie B. Barkin is killed and goes to heaven. Even though he's told that if he goes back to Earth, he can't return to heaven, he feels he has to return to rescue an orphan girl who talks to animals.

DOGGY TIP

If your dog falls in love with one special toy that gets grosser by the day, try this trick: Buy a toy as much like the old one as possible. Wrap the shreds of the old toy around the new one to give it the same scent. After the dog has accepted the new toy, throw away the pieces of the old one!

The Adventures of Milo and Otis – Otis the pug and Milo the kitten survive all kinds of harrowing experiences together in this film that was originally made for Japanese television.

Babe – Babe the piglet is adopted by a friendly dog and decides that in order to avoid becoming dinner, he'd better become useful and learn how to herd sheep just like a dog. (The script was based on a children's book, and the story is partly true!)

Balto – Based on a true story from the 1920s, a half-dog, half-wolf named Balto becomes a hero when he brings medication to sick children in the wilderness of Alaska.

Eight Below – Real-life events in 1957 inspired the filmmakers of this adventure movie. A team of sled dogs are forced to survive alone in Antarctica for six months after the scientists who brought them there must leave them behind.

Air Bud – This Disney comedy features a dog, Buddy, who plays basketball better than anyone on the school's team, helping his shy owner, Josh, make new friends. (Buddy the

My Dog Story

"I made a very cool plaster cast of my dog's paw-print. After he stepped in the soft ground and made a good print, I took a strip of cardboard, taped the ends to make a circle, and pressed it into the ground around the paw-print. I mixed plaster of Paris (2 cups) and water (5 cups), and poured it into the cardboard frame. It hardened in a couple of minutes, and I rinsed off the mud."

—Josh

dog was discovered by the film's producers when he was featured on *Late Show with David Letterman*'s "Stupid Pet Tricks" segment.)

Snow Dogs – A dentist from Miami and his stubborn team of sled dogs face off against rough-and-tumble racing veterans as they trek across Alaska.

Turner and Hooch – When a local man is murdered, Turner, the detective on the case, discovers that the only witness to the crime was the victim's dog Hooch. Turner, who is no dog lover, is forced to work with Hooch to solve the case.

Zeus and Roxanne – Zeus is a dog, Roxanne a dolphin. Marine biologist Mary Beth is fascinated by the friendship and decides to study it. Meanwhile, the villain, another researcher named Claude, tries to steal her work.

Cats and Dogs – This comedy uses live action, animation, and puppetry to explain the age-old fight between cats and dogs. Apparently, dogs have been defending humans to keep cats from taking over the planet. Mr. Tinkles (a cat) has to go up against a tough pack of dogs if he wants to rule the world.

The Shaggy Dog – The 2006 movie is a remake of a 1959 favorite in which a teenage boy keeps turning into a sheepdog.

Beethoven – When a family takes in a stray Saint Bernard puppy, they never imagined how their lives would change as he grew ... and grew ... and grew! An evil veterinarian continuously tries to steal their pet in order to perform lab experiments on him.

Underdog – Based on the classic cartoon, this movie follows the adventures of a beagle who suddenly discovers he has superpowers. He must use them to save the city—and his favorite pooch pal, Polly.

A Doggone Great Movie

Do you get the sense that your dog would like to watch a movie intended just for him? *The Movie for Dogs* was made so that dogs would not be lonely when their owners were gone. It is over an hour long, but is programmed to repeat itself so that it will play again and again. Your pet will love watching dogs jumping, playing, swimming, and competing, and will love the dog soundtrack too! (A lot of pet owners enjoy watching the movie with their dogs!)

You can order the movie through the web site *www.themoviefordogs.com*, or check out the list of store locations on the site.

If you are resourceful, and your family has a video camera, you can make your own dog movie. You know exactly what your dog likes, so start filming! Head to a local dog show, to a dog park, the beach, or anyplace where you'll be able to take a video of dogs having fun. Don't forget to include footage of your own dog and his antics.

To make a DVD that's top notch, check out computer programs that will allow you to edit your footage and use graphics like a real movie producer.

Adventures with Your Dog

There are all sorts of interesting things for a boy and dog to do together. Some of

Pup Quiz

What do the dogs Hercules, Laddy, and Santa's Little Helper have in common?

a. all have appeared on the TV show *The Simpsons*

b. all have piloted an airplane

c. all can do cartwheels, according to the *Guinness World Records* book

Answer: a

them depend on what kind of dog you have or where you live. Read on to find the perfect activity for you and your dog!

Hiking

Dogs make great hiking companions! You'll need to do a little planning before you head for the trail, though. Be sure that the route you're taking permits dogs. If you're taking a long hike, check a map ahead of time to be sure there aren't any places that would be dangerous for your dog (or you). Bring a leash for the dog and drinking water for both of you (and a collapsible bowl for your dog to drink from). You can even get a dog backpack so that your pooch carries his own stuff!

If you're hiking during hunting season, both you and your dog should wear orange reflective vests while you're in the woods. The website *www.youractivepet.com* features all sorts of outdoor gear for your pup.

When you're hiking, try to keep your dog one step behind you. This is the safest place for her. You want to be the one to spot the porcupine or the skunk first!

For loads of info about this activity, check out *www.hikewithyourdog.com*.

Biking

So that she can safely trot beside you while you ride a bike, your dog needs to know the commands "Heel" and "Stop." (You can watch a video on teaching your dog to heel at *www.expertvillage.com*. Look up "heel command, dog obedience training." For "Stop," read the heel/stop advice on *www.pbs.org/wgbh/woof/tips/tip_08.html*.) She also needs to be able to ignore cats, squirrels, other dogs, and cars.

Work up to a regular bike ride by first pushing your bike as she walks beside you, then riding slowly.

A word of caution: It's tricky to have the dog on a leash while you ride because she may pull you over. You may want to check out a product designed especially for dogs jogging beside bikes called a Springer (see *www.dog-training.com/springer.htm*).

If your dog can't keep up with you or won't stay next to you when you ride, consider getting a basket that attaches to your handlebars (for a smaller dog), or using a bicycle trailer that attaches to the back. The trailers are made for kids who want to ride with their parents, but are perfect for smaller dogs.

Swimming

Get your pup familiar with water by starting him off in a backyard wading pool. Also, get him used to wearing a doggy life vest by putting it on him at home for short periods of time. Reward him for letting you put it on.

When it's time to introduce him to a lake, find one with a gentle slope to the water, and let *him* decide if and when he wants to go in. If possible, bring along a dog that already likes water—peer pressure!

While you're teaching your dog to go into the water, you should wear a life vest, too. A dog that panics might try to climb onto you.

To start, stand in knee-deep water and toss a few treats into the water and encourage the dog to come and get them. Once the dog feels more comfortable in the water, you can take off his life vest.

Remember: Some dogs, like bulldogs, might not be able to

swim (bulldogs can actually drown easily), so don't push your dog to do something he's not comfortable doing.

Camping

It's best to try camping in your backyard before heading to a campground or into the woods. Set up your tent behind your house and have a practice overnight. Not only will this get your dog used to the experience, but you'll have a chance to see if you've forgotten to pack anything (with your house just a few feet away!).

You'll need to bring items from your day-hike list, and anything you'd bring to camp out with your human friends, as well as a rope or tether to tie your dog at night, a dog bed (and a piece of plastic to place under it), and dog food.

Check out *www.coyotecom.com/dogcamp.html* for all the info you need to know about canine camping.

Over-the-Top Adventures

Sledding

Are you looking for something a little more unusual to do with your dog? How about dog sledding? You don't need a typical sled dog, just a dog that weighs between 40 and 60 pounds and loves to pull. (You don't even need snow! There are special sleds made with wheels, that work in places where it doesn't snow.)

A kick sled, which is a light chair on runners, is made to be

Doggy Summer Camp

Did you know that you can take your dog to summer camp? Check out these web sites for information about camps near you:

www.dogplay.com/ Activities/camps.html

www.dogpatch.org/ doginfo/camp.html

pushed by a person, but it could be pulled by one or two dogs. Other types of sleds are made for a team of dogs. Dogs wear harnesses that are attached to the sled with "gang lines." You can check out *www.sleddogcentral.com* for more details.

Be patient as you get your dog used to the harness and then used to pulling a small cart or sled. If you know of someone who has an experienced sled dog, see if he and his dog would like to help teach your dog the ropes.

Carting

If you don't live in snow country, you might be able to teach your large dog to pull you in a cart!

You'll need to invest in a harness and a cart, probably a two-wheeled cart with a seat. Begin by getting the dog used to

Weird dog fact

The Iditarod has been called The Last Great Race on Earth. Teams of sled dogs race more than 1,150 miles from Anchorage to Nome, Alaska along the Iditarod Trail, over mountain ranges, across frozen rivers, through forests, and across desolate plains. They race in harsh winds that make it hard to see, during long stretches of darkness, in temperatures well below zero. The race takes anywhere from 10 to 17 days.

In 1925, teams of sled dogs and mushers used the Iditarod Trail to bring life-saving medicine to Nome, which was facing a diphtheria epidemic. The Iditarod race commemorates that event.

the harness. Once he's comfortable, attach him to the empty cart and lead him around the yard. Use lots of praise and treats! Add weight to the cart very gradually, until he can pull something that weighs about as much as you do.

Your best Internet resource for carting is *www.cartingwithyourdog.com*.

For both of these activities, your dog will need to know the "Pull" command. Read up on how to teach your pup at *www.skijornow.com/pull. html*.

Going for the Gold!

There are fun and games, and then there are competitive fun and games! A dog sport can involve all sorts of things, from obstacle courses or hurdles to a flying disc or ball.

The American Kennel Club (AKC) organizes dog shows and events, including junior showmanship classes for kids aged 9 to 18. The Novice class for juniors is great for beginners. If you've taken some classes or lessons with your dog and think he has what it takes to win, you can attend a dog show and talk to some of the kids who compete. The AKC web site (*www.akc.org*) lists upcoming events in your area. You can also check out the *AKC Jr. News*, an e-newsletter for kids interested in competing. To get an idea of what's involved, you can read past issues on the AKC site.

If your dog isn't a purebred, check out *mbdca.tripod.com*, the web site for the Mixed Breed Dog Clubs of America. This group sponsors competitions for mixed-breed dogs in obedience, tracking, conformation, and other categories.

Here are just a few dog sports for you to consider:

Agility: Basically an obstacle course for dogs, an agility competition rewards accuracy and speed. And for those of you with tiny dogs, don't worry, your dog will compete against dogs in the same size range. No Chihuahua versus German shepherd events here!

To get more information, check out the AKC site, as well as the site for the United States Agility Association: *www.usdaa.com*.

Conformation: Like Miss Universe, but for dogs. In this competition, each dog is judged by comparing him to the "standard" for his breed, which is a description of the ideal dog of that breed. Most winning dogs were bred to be show dogs.

Obedience: If your perfect little pup follows directions well, you may want to enter him in an obedience competition. He'll be judged on how well he obeys commands, some as complicated as following a scent trail or responding to hand signals. A relatively new type of competition called rally combines obedience and agility and is a great first event for kids who are new to dog sports. Log onto *www.akc.org* and

Weird Dog Fact
A dog named Laika was the first living creature to orbit the earth. On November 3, 1957, she headed into space on the Soviet Union's Sputnik 2. (Sadly, they weren't able to bring her back to Earth, so she died in space.)

click on "kids/juniors" for information about competitions.

Tracking: Does your dog have a nose that works overtime? Tracking may be her sport! She'll have to be able to track a human scent and find a specific article—even if that means crossing rivers, fences, or other obstacles. It's a pass/fail event.

For more info, check out *www.abtc.org/tracking*.

Flyball: If you're an extreme sports fan, this may be the sport for you and your dog! It involves hurdles, catching balls in the air, and a four-dog relay team. Even though each race lasts less than a minute, training for the sport might take six months! Teaching your dog to fetch and jump over hurdles is the first step. You'll want to recruit a fast, short dog for your team because the hurdles will be lowered to accommodate the smallest teammate, making it easier for the big boys! You can learn more at *www.flyball.org*.

Flying Discs: For dogs who love to jump up and snatch plastic discs out of the air, check out this cool sport! Any dog, not just a purebred, can compete. Dogs are scored on the distance and difficulty of each catch. You can begin training your dog by rolling a Frisbee® to him, then try throwing it so that it isn't far off the ground and isn't aimed directly at him. Log onto *www.iddha.com* for more info.

Dock diving: Dock diving is a relatively new type of organized sport for dogs and their owners, and it's catching on fast. Any breed, from the smallest Chihuahua to the largest Great Dane, can compete against others in its class to see which dog jumps the farthest off a dock—usually jumping after a favorite toy! The dogs love it, and owners do too. For more information and a list of events in your area, check out *www.dockdogs.com*.

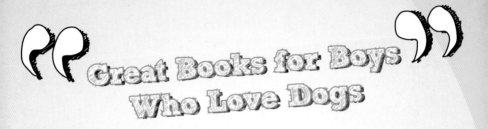

Great Books for Boys Who Love Dogs

Ages 5-8

***Walter the Farting Dog* series, by William Kotzwinkle and Glenn Murray.** A farting dog that saves the day with his little, uh, problem—what could be more fun for a boy to read about?

***Dog Breath*, by Dav Pilkey.** If a dog saving the day with his farts doesn't appeal to you, how about one who saves the day with his bad breath?

The *Pinkerton* series of books, by Steven Kellogg. A Great Dane manages to get into (and eventually out of) all sorts of crazy trouble.

***Bad Dog, Marley!* by John Grogan.** As Marley, the Labrador puppy, gets bigger, so do the problems he creates!

The *Henry and Mudge* series, by Cynthia Rylant. Henry and his dog, Mudge, have all sorts of adventures in these short, easy-to-read early chapter books.

***The Bravest Dog Ever: The True Story of Balto*, by Natalie Standiford.** This easy-to-read book tells the inspiring story of the sled dog that, in 1925, led his dog team more than 50 miles to deliver medicine.

Ages 9 to 12

***The Good Dog*, by Avi.** Lots of action and a tale of leadership told from the dog's point of view make this a story that dog-loving boys will devour.

***Red Dog*, by Bill Wallace.** Set in the 1860s, this book tells a gripping tale of Adam and his dog. A fast-paced plot, lots of adventure, and a good-over-evil ending make this a great read.

***Shelter Dogs: Amazing Stories of Adopted Strays*, by Peg Kehret.** If you prefer nonfiction, you'll love these true stories of unwanted dogs that survived and thrived.

The *Hank the Cowdog* series, by John R. Erickson and Gerald L. Holmes. Hank is big on confidence and small on brains, so he manages to get tangled up in all sorts of crazy situations.

***Along Came a Dog*, by Meindert Dejong.** Boys will love this award-winning story about a lonely dog and the hen he befriends, told from both points of view.

***My Life in Dog Years*, by Gary Paulsen.** Paulsen tells the true stories of dogs who've been part of his life, from a sled dog that saved him to a Great Dane that was scared of Halloween.

***Shiloh*, by Phyllis Reynolds Naylor.** This is the classic story of an 11-year-old boy who finds an abused dog and must decide what to do.

***Snow Dog*, by Jim Kjelgaard.** Your dad may have read this as a boy! It's the story of a dog left alone in the wild who befriends a trapper, and lives in fear of the black wolf that killed his family.

***Where the Red Fern Grows*, by Wilson Rawls.** This classic story of a boy and his pups and their adventures in the Ozarks of Oklahoma has moved kids for almost 50 years.

***Greatest Dog Stories*, by Fred Gipson and William H. Armstrong.** Three timeless novels are combined in one book: *Old Yeller*, *Sounder*, and *Savage Sam*.

***Help! I'm Trapped in Obedience School*, by Todd Strasser.** Imagine the adventures that would result from a boy and his dog switching bodies!

Chapter 11

Your Healthy, Happy Dog A healthy dog is a happy dog. You have the power to keep your dog healthy by offering him good food and clean water, brushing him regularly, giving him enough exercise, and taking him to the vet for checkups and shots.

Choosing a Vet

You and your parents can ask people you trust to share the names of good veterinarians. Your parents can call and ask to meet with the vet to see if it's going to be a good fit. You want a vet whose office is clean, who is easy to talk to, and who is skilled with animals. The vet should take plenty of time with you, answer all of your questions, and explain things in a way that you understand. She should be able to help your pet relax and treat him kindly.

Visiting the Vet

Your dog will probably get very excited at the vet's office—all of those new animal smells and maybe even a few dogs or cats in the waiting room! Bring his favorite toy and encourage him to lie down next to your chair while you wait. Bring some treats, and give a few to the receptionist and the vet so that they can hand them to your puppy when he behaves well.

Checkups and Vaccines

DOGGY TIP

There are a few ways you can help the vet. Work with your dog so that he's used to being handled the way the vet does. Before an appointment, jot down notes about your pet, such as if he's been eating, drinking, and pooping normally. Remind the vet if your dog has had certain problems because she might not remember. Finally, ask questions until you understand exactly what the vet is telling you.

Take your pup in to see a vet as soon as you can. The vet will put your dog on a schedule for his vaccinations so that he doesn't miss an important shot.

Puppies get their first shots at about six weeks. Some shots—like rabies—are required by law, and others, like the

shot to prevent Lyme disease, are recommended for the dog's health. In some cases, your dog's health can affect your family, so making sure he gets his shots will protect you as well.

You should take the dog in once a year for a physical, just like you see the pediatrician once a year. Dogs age faster than people do, so taking a dog in once a year is like you going to the doctor every five to eight years!

It's easier to prevent health problems than to fix them, so the vet will help you see that your pooch stays in good shape.

"Fixing" your pup

When your pup is six months old, you and your parents will decide whether to spay her or neuter him. When a male dog is neutered, his testicles are removed and he can no longer father a litter. When a female dog is spayed, her reproductive system—her uterus, fallopian tubes, and ovaries—are removed and she cannot get pregnant with puppies. "Fixing" may seem like a cruel or unnecessary thing to do, but it isn't. Not only will it prevent more unwanted puppies in the world, but it keeps male dogs from wandering off

Weird Dog Fact
Studies have shown that dogs relax more and bark less when they listen to classical music. So turn down the Jay-Z, and turn up the Mozart!

Pup Quiz
True or false: Your dog can catch your cold, and you can catch his.

Answer: False

and aggressively seeking mates, and it prevents certain cancers. Female dogs are protected from many cancers, as well as from unneutered males who might come into the yard. Have your parents talk to your vet for guidance.

Pet stores and the vet's office sell special tweezers designed for removing ticks from dogs.

Fleas and ticks

In Chapter 5, we discussed how to determine whether your dog has fleas and how to treat and prevent them. Monthly applications such as Frontline® during flea and tick season work well to prevent problems. Your mom or dad can talk to the vet about the best and safest products to keep your dog pest-free.

Ticks are dangerous because they carry disease. Brown ticks can transmit Rocky Mountain spotted fever, and deer ticks can carry Lyme disease, dangerous to both dogs and humans. A tick might be the size of a tiny speck, or the size of a pea—how large or small it is will vary, according to its life stage and species.

If you find a tick on your dog, you'll probably need your mom or dad to help you. It's tricky for one person to remove a tick from a squirming dog, and it's best left to an adult. First, your parent should soak a cotton ball in rubbing alcohol and press it against the tick. Then he should carefully remove the tick with a pair of tweezers by grabbing the head of the tick and pulling up and out. The tick can be disposed of by putting it into a small jar filled with rubbing alcohol.

Doggone Funny
Q: Where should you never take a dog?
A: To a flea market!

Worms

Tapeworms, hookworms, heartworms; your dog can have quite a variety of worm-related conditions—and some of them can be transmitted to kids! The veterinarian will tell you what tests will detect worms, what symptoms you should watch for (loss of appetite or bloody poops, for example) and what kinds of medication the dog can take if she gets worms.

Heartworms are particularly deadly for dogs, and most vets recommend that dogs take a pill regularly to prevent them. Vets also recommend a yearly test to make sure the dog does not have heartworms.

Weird Dog Fact

Dogs have three eyelids! They have an upper one, a lower one, and an extra one inside the other two. If that's not weird enough, the third eyelid is called a "haw."

Ear Infections

If you've ever had an ear infection, you know that they are painful. Some dogs get them often. Suggest that your parents call the vet if you notice the dog has red or swollen ears, scratches at his ears or shakes his head a lot, or has ear discharge or odor. The vet will prescribe an ointment that you'll put in the dog's ears at home.

Doggy Breath

By taking care of your dog's teeth, you can help prevent doggy breath. You can keep his teeth clean by brushing them using special dog toothbrushes and toothpaste sold at pet stores. (Dogs will get sick if you use toothpaste meant for people.)

Vets recommend brushing twice a week. Begin by brushing a couple of teeth at a time. Soon, the dog will allow you to brush them all. Use the same circular motion you use for your own teeth.

Brushing is also a good time to check out the dog's teeth and gums. Gums should be pink and firm, and his teeth should be white all the way to the gum line.

You can also try buying toys made to help his teeth stay clean. Cotton-rope chews keep teeth and gums healthy. Also look for nylon toys that have raised bumps designed for dental health.

Doggy Farts

The only positive thing about a dog that has a problem with gas is that you can blame any gas of your own on the dog, and everyone will believe you. But that's the ONLY positive thing!

If your dog is a farter, check his diet to be sure he's not taking in too much meat, too many gas-inducing foods like onions or beans, or too much dairy. Read the list of ingredients on his dog-food bag. Your vet might recommend a better food for him, and you can slowly move him over to his new diet.

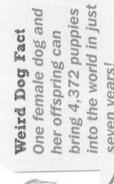

Weird Dog Fact
One female dog and her offspring can bring 4,372 puppies into the world in just seven years!

When to Call the Vet

Just as your parents know when to call the pediatrician for you, you will probably know when the

> I love dogs—
> sometimes more
> than humans.
> —Simon Cowell

vet needs to be called for your dog. You will sense it if your dog is acting different from the way he normally does. Maybe he's not eating or drinking as much, or maybe he seems unusually tired.

Even smellier breath can be a sign that the dog is sick! Or it could be more obvious, such as if he is making choking noises, has severe diarrhea or vomiting, is bleeding, or is exhibiting very strange behavior.

Obviously, you'll want to call the vet right away if the dog is hit by a car, has been in a fight with another animal, has eaten something poisonous, or has suffered any type of accident. Until you are able to get him to the vet's office, keep him still and warm, and comfort him quietly.

Learn the signs of a healthy dog: a clean, shiny coat; clear eyes; ears that do not have a bad odor; a nose that doesn't run; and a fit body. Your pooch should have plenty of energy and a good appetite.

Keep Your Dog's Environment Clean

Your mom or dad washes the sheets on your bed, and it's important to make sure your dog's bed stays clean, too. If it has a removable outside cover, wash it at least every week or so.

Weird Dog Fact

The "dog days" are the hot, sticky days of July and August. That's the time of year when Sirius—the "dog star," and the brightest star in the sky—rises and sets with the sun. The ancient Romans believed that the heat from Sirius combined with the sun's heat to make those days unbearably hot.

Also be sure to clean up the area where he spends most of his time outside. You don't want him to get dog poop on his paws and then jump onto your bed! That's not healthy for either of you.

Holiday Safety

Did you know that more dogs disappear on the Fourth of July than on any other day? Many dogs are spooked by the fireworks and run away. That's a day to keep your pooch on a leash if he's outside, or in a room with soothing music playing if he's inside, especially if he's been fearful of loud noises before.

Halloween is another day that might not be your dog's favorite. Even if he's normally friendly to guests, the constant stream of visitors to the house in strange costumes might make him anxious. During trick-or-treating hours, he's best off in your room with some of his favorite toys.

Holidays like Easter and Valentine's Day can be dangerous for dogs, too, because holiday chocolates can make them very sick. Be sure to keep any kind of chocolate up high where your dog can't get to it.

Also, don't be tempted to share turkey bones with your pup on Thanksgiving. They can splinter like chicken bones and injure his insides or make him choke.

Christmas is full of hidden dangers for your dog, from the tinsel and other things he might eat off the tree, to poisonous holiday plants like mistletoe, poinsettia, and holly. Talk to your parents about how you can protect your pup from these holiday dangers.

Things That Can Stress Your Dog

Change is stressful for dogs, even if the change is good, like moving to a bigger house with a huge yard. To a dog, comfort is things staying the same. He knows where and when he will be fed, and where you are likely to be when he's looking for you. When dogs are confused or upset, they sometimes react by doing things like barking, nipping, acting wild, or even withdrawing.

Moving

If you are about to move to a new home, make things as familiar as possible for your pup. Even if his old bed has gotten dirty and gross, bring it along and use it for the first few weeks. Favorite toys, food bowls, and treats will help him to settle in more easily. Don't let him off the leash after you move until you're sure he knows where home is.

A New Baby

Another source of anxiety for a dog is the arrival of a new baby in the family. Before the baby comes home, you can get your dog used to little children by taking him to playgrounds or visiting friends who have little brothers or sisters. If your parents have bought new toys for the baby, put a dab of mouthwash on each one, and tell your dog "No!" if he tries to chew on one. Soon he'll understand that mouthwash means "No!"

Before the baby comes home, bring blankets or sheets from the hospital to put in the baby's nursery to get the dog used to the scent. If you can have the dog meet the baby on neutral ground, like in the parking lot at the hospital, the dog won't feel territorial. You'll have to remind your parents not to use "good boy!" with both the dog and the baby. Your pup will get confused!

A New Pet

Bringing another dog into the family, while it is exciting for you, can be very a stressful situation for the dog you already have. Try to have the dogs meet for the first time in a park or other neutral territory so that they can get used to each other.

You'll have to let them figure out which is the dominant dog, and you have to go along with their decision! Don't interfere if the top dog ends up with both of the bones you bought. If they get into a serious fight, spray them with the hose; if it's not serious, walk away. Using their pack instincts, the dogs will work things out if you let them.

Hot Dogs

Summer is lots of fun for boys as well as their dogs, but both can get overheated. The difference is that dogs can't let you know when they're too hot, and they don't have a very good body-cooling system. Black dogs and those with long or thick coats are at greatest risk of suffering from heat-related stress to their bodies.

Weird Dog Fact
Dogs sweat through the pads on their feet!

Here are some great ways to help your dog beat the heat:

• Buy a kiddie pool and set it up in the shade so your pooch can take a cool dip.

• Make your dog a "pupsicle." Pour low-sodium chicken broth into an empty yogurt container and put it in your freezer. When you want to give it to your dog, pour warm water on the sides of the container so that the frozen broth slides out easily.

• Make chicken-broth ice cubes, drop them into an old sock, and tie a knot at the open end—half toy, half treat!

• Let your dog stand or sleep on a wet towel. Because dogs cool from the bottom up, they are better off on top of a cool, wet towel than under one!

• Let her run through the lawn sprinkler (or if she's afraid, toss a ball through the spray and she'll chase it). Splash cool water on her stomach and paws.

• Place a frozen water bottle (without the top) in her outside bed.

• Cut off the bottom of a milk or orange-juice jug, fill it with water, add a handful of treats, and put it in the freezer. Your dog will have a blast licking the melting ice to get at the treats!

Chilly Dogs

Remember these tips for keeping your pooch happy and healthy on the coldest days.

• It's best not to let your dog off the leash when there's snow on the ground, especially during a storm. He may not be able to follow a scent in the snow and may get lost.

• Your pup will be very grateful if you wipe off her paws when she comes in from the cold. The salt that is put on the roads in the winter will make her sick if she licks it off of her paws. Better yet, use old socks as booties for your pup before she goes outside. (Dog booties available online and in pet stores offer the best cold-weather protection for your dog's feet.)

Weird Dog Fact
Six out of 10 dog owners have little coats or sweaters for their pets.

• You may not want to parade him around in front of your friends while he's wearing it, but you should buy your dog a sweater if he has very short hair and you plan on spending long stretches outside with him.

• Heat pads made to be warmed in the microwave will keep your dog's bed warm for hours on cold nights. Have your mom or dad ask at your local pet store about products than can help keep your buddy cozy on chilly nights.

• Dogs are sometimes tempted to lick antifreeze that can drip from the underside of a car. Keep your dog away if you ever notice any puddles (the fluid is sometimes a yellowish-green), as licking even a few drops of this is deadly for pets.

Dog Libs

Fill out the list below, then plug in the words in the right places as you read the paragraph on the next page. (Or if you have a brother or friend handy, you can ask him to tell you what kinds of words are needed to fill in the blanks, and he can write down your answers. Then he can read it to you when you're finished!)

Just for reminders, an adjective describes a thing (*squishy, smelly, wiggly*); a noun is a person, place, or thing (*chin, bump, caboose*); and a plural noun is more than one thing. An example of an exclamation would be "Yikes!" or "Wow!"

Have fun!

_____ *plural noun*	_____ *body part, plural*
_____ *adjective*	_____ *number*
_____ *body part, plural*	_____ *animal, plural*
_____ *adjective*	_____ *adjective*
_____ *color*	_____ *adjective*
_____ *color*	_____ *adjective*
_____ *adjective*	_____ *exclamation*

The American Hairless Terrier

Have you ever seen a dog without _____? The American hairless ter-
[plural noun]
rier is a _____ breed that is completely hairless except for small tufts
[adjective]
of hair on the _____. Even though these dogs are hairless, they have
[body part, plural]
_____ whiskers. Their skin is usually pink with _____ or _____ spots.
[adjective]   [color]   [color]
The puppies are born with _____ hair all over their _____, but they
[adjective]   [body part, plural]
shed this fuzz by the time they are _____ weeks old. Also, unlike other
[number]
_____, American hairless terriers will break out into a sweat when
[animal, plural]
they are _____ or scared! Many people think these dogs are very
[adjective]
_____ but others are so _____ to see a hairless dog that they may
[adjective]   [adjective]
shout: _____!
[exclamation]

In the box below, draw the dog you described in your dog lib.

Now turn the page to see a drawing of an American hairless
terrier. How different is your dog from the drawing?

Want to try drawing it again?

Chapter 12

Throw Your Pup a Party! Birthday parties aren't just for kids! In fact, pet parties are becoming more and more popular. Here are some ideas for celebrating your dog's big day.

The Plan

You can have the party in your back yard, or find another dog-friendly spot! If you have the party at home, you need to have a fenced-in yard, with a way to get into the yard without having to go through the house. The party should last about an hour so that the dogs don't get too excited and tired out.

If you don't have a good yard for a party, think about having the party somewhere else. You could have the party at a beach (off-season) or a dog park (visit *www.dogpark.com* to find a park near you). Many businesses that cater to pets—like dog grooming salons, dog daycare places, or dog training schools—also offer dog party packages. They will run the party for you, plan activities, and handle any problems that might come up. These parties can be expensive, maybe $40 or higher, so you and your parents will have to decide how much to spend.

Invitations

Send an e-vite, buy invitations online (*www.funstufffordogs.com*), or make your own. You can cut out a dog bone or fire hydrant shape, or make one that looks like a dog house, with a door that opens to reveal the 411.

If you don't mind paying a little extra postage (and writing "Hand Cancel" on the envelope), you can include a dog biscuit with each invite!

The Guest List

Invite dogs that your dog already knows and likes. Your best bet is to invite dogs that are about the same age as yours, are good-natured, and a mix of males and females. If some dogs are not spayed or neutered, you'll need to let everyone know. (Some of your friends might not want a litter of puppies as a party favor!)

Don't forget about the humans! Invite kids you know will like one another and enjoy a dog party. You can also invite friends who don't have dogs but are dog lovers; they could be a big help.

Themes and Decorations

Just about any theme that works for a kid party works for a dog party. You could have a circus party in which the dogs show off their tricks, or a costume party where the dogs come in crazy outfits. For a beach party, put out a wading pool, a pile of sand for digging, and flying discs.

Your local dollar store will have paper streamers and balloons, or you can get fancy and order paw-print balloons from *www.doggonegood.com*. For other puppy party supplies, check out *www.tailwagging.com* or *www.funstufffordogs.com*.

DOGGY TIP: When you're taking photos of the dogs at your party, get down at "dog level" for the best pics. Pay attention to the background, too. You want it as simple as possible—a fence or shrubs, for instance. You may want to ask someone to stand behind you and engage the dog, telling him to sit or getting his attention with a squeaky toy.

Fun and Games

Games with balls, both large and small, flying discs, and other toys can be fun with a group of dogs, as long as none of the dogs is too aggressive. There are lots of organized games you can play, too.

• You can have a game to see whose dog is the best trained. Which dog will sit and then stay the longest, as each of you backs away from your pet?

• Musical chairs, doggy style, requires several party guests.

Humans walk their pets around the yard until the music stops, then each one tries to make his dog sit before the others. The last one to sit is out for that round.

- If your mom or dad doesn't mind holding all of the dogs on leashes at one end of the yard, the dog owners can line up on the other end. At the signal, the leashes are released and the dogs are called by name. The first one to reach his owner is the winner!

- Bobbing for hot dogs is a popular party game for four-legged partiers. Cut hot dogs into bite-sized pieces and float them in a tub of water. Give each dog two minutes to see how many he can get!

- Make a tub of popcorn (without salt or butter). Have the dogs sit a few feet from their owners. Toss kernels of popcorn to the dogs, and see which dog catches the most kernels out of the air in two minutes.

You could even invite or hire a special guest who is a dog expert, like someone who trains dogs and can teach the party guests a new trick or two.

Food and Water

Put water in a large container and keep it filled. Food shouldn't be put out until you're ready for the dogs to eat. Each dog owner should feed his own dog, using commands like "Sit" and "Stay" if they have trained their dogs, and holding them on their leashes if they haven't. Make sure the dogs are fed small, one-

Good Doggy Deed

If you want to help the dogs at your local animal shelter, call and find out what their needs are. Rather than gifts, you can ask each guest to bring a can or bag of dog food, an old blanket or towel, or something else that the homeless dogs can use.

gulp bites. If one dog is gnawing on a big treat, the other dogs might go after it, resulting in a party-stopping dog fight!

As for the birthday cake, you have a few choices. You can buy one at a local dog bakery or you can make one yourself, from a dog cake mix or from scratch. In any case, remember that dog cakes are for dogs, and human cakes are for humans!

Don't forget about the hungry humans at your party. You can make PB&J or ham and cheese sandwiches, and then use a bone-shaped cookie cutter so the food fits the theme. Arrange for everyone to go inside for people food, but set up the snacks so that you can see outside to keep track of all the dogs.

After the party

Send everyone home with dog biscuits tied up in a cool bandana that the dog can wear. Post the party photos on a web site for everyone to enjoy!

Turn to the next page for a recipe for birthday party "pup" cakes! (Thanks to Jessica Disbrow Talley, author of *The Organic Dog Biscuit Cookbook* and co-owner of a wholesome dog-treat bakery in Rockaway, New Jersey, called the Bubba Rose Biscuit Company!)

Gift Tips
If you're the one invited to a puppy party, here are some great gift ideas:
- a coupon for a weekend of dog-sitting or dog-walking
- pigs' ears or pigs' hooves
- homemade dog treats (see pages 39–40)
- dog goggles for pups that like to stick their heads out the window
- a reflective collar or harness for dogs that go out at night

"Because I Carob 'Bout You" Pup Cakes

You may want to bake these in mini-muffin pans because then dogs won't be as likely to overdo the sweet treats!

For the pupcakes:
1 c. oat flour*
1 c. brown rice flour*
2 tsp. baking soda
½ tsp. baking powder
¼ c. carob powder (can not be substituted with chocolate)
1 egg
2 Tb. honey
¼ c. water
¼ c. safflower oil
½ c. plain non-fat yogurt

For icing (optional):
1 c. banana, mashed & pureed
1 8-oz. package non-fat cream cheese (at room temperature)
1 tsp. vanilla

*All-purpose flour or whole wheat flour may be used instead of oat flour or brown rice flour.

Preheat the oven to 350°. Combine all the ingredients and mix them thoroughly. Place paper liners in a mini muffin pan (or a regular muffin pan). Spoon the mixture evenly into the liners, filling them to the top (the mix will not rise very much).

Bake for 10 to 15 minutes if you're using the mini-muffin pan, or 20 to 25 minutes if you're using a regular-sized muffin pan. The cupcakes are done when a toothpick inserted into the center comes out clean. Remove them from the oven and let them cool completely on a wire rack.

Peel, mash, and puree the banana for the frosting. In a separate bowl, combine the icing ingredients and mix them thoroughly. Decorate the mini cupcakes. Store them in an airtight container in the refrigerator.

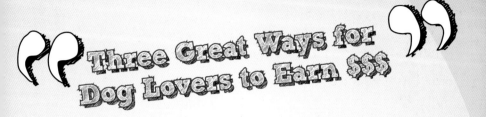

- **Have a dog wash.** Advertise ahead of time, set up your dog wash in a central location, and be sure to have helpers and all the supplies you need. Ask the dog owners to wait while you wash, just in case. (This is a great fund-raising event for your school, sports team, or Boy Scout troop.)

- **Set up a dog walking business.** Send out flyers to people within walking distance of your house or school. You can probably charge about $8 per walk, and might be able to walk a few dogs at a time! Be sure all the dogs have up-to-date vaccinations and are used to being leash-walked.

- **Offer after-school doggie day care.** People who work late often need someone to feed and water their dogs or let their dogs out. Or they may just want someone to come and play with their pups so they don't get lonely. You can charge by the hour for this service; find out what the babysitters in your neighborhood are being paid and use that as a guideline.

Chapter 13

Top Dog Dogs are smart! After all, think of the amazing things they do, from searching for illegal drugs in airports to leading blind people around city streets! How does your dog compare to other dogs? Is he smarter or not quite as bright? How about when you compare him to your best friend? Then how does he stack up? In this case, maybe it's not "How smart are you?" but rather "How are you smart?" Dogs and people have different kinds of intelligence! Read on to learn all about dogs and their amazing brains!

Ways to Test How Smart Your Dog Really Is!

Do you think your dog is especially smart? The Albert Einstein of the canine world? Well, there are several ways to test your dog's intelligence. Dog experts say that the best way is to see how well a dog can solve a problem. Another way is to see how long a dog works at solving a problem. If he keeps trying to figure something out, he is considered smarter than a dog that gives up easily.

> Cats are smarter than dogs. You can't get eight cats to pull a sled through snow.
>
> **—Jeff Valdez**

Many people assume a dog that is able to learn a lot of tricks is smart. The experts aren't sure whether this is true, but a dog who can shake hands and roll over when he's told to will make your friends think he's smart!

Here's one common dog I.Q. test you can try out on your pet. You'll need a stopwatch, a towel, two treats, three buckets, a paper towel, a box, his leash, and a dog toy.

Part One:

Toss a large towel over your dog's head.

Scoring:

3 points if he frees himself from the towel in under 15 seconds

2 points if he frees himself in 15 to 30 seconds

1 point if he frees himself in more than 30 seconds

Part Two:

Line up three upside-down buckets. Put a yummy treat under one of them. Show your dog which bucket is over the treat. Walk the dog away from the buckets for about ten steps.

Then turn him back toward the buckets and let him go.

Scoring:

> 3 points if he goes directly to the bucket hiding the treat
>
> 2 points if he gets it on the second try
>
> 1 point if it takes him three tries to get it right (and that's kind of a gift point, to be honest)

Part Three:

Put a treat on a piece of paper towel. Fold the towel over twice to cover the treat.

Scoring:

> 3 points if the dog uses his paws like hands to get to the treat
>
> 2 points if he uses his mouth as well as his paws
>
> 1 point if he plays with the wrapped treat but can't open it

Part Four:

Cut the sides and bottom of a large carton and open it to make a barricade. Cut a slit in the box, and place a favorite toy behind the slit where the dog can see it but can't get to it. Urge the dog to get to the toy.

Scoring:

> 3 points if it takes less than 15 seconds for the dog to go around the barrier and get the toy
>
> 2 points if it takes between 15 and 30 seconds
>
> 1 point if it takes longer or if the dog tries to get at the toy through the slit

Make a noise so that your dog looks at you. Without saying anything else, pick up his leash and walk to the middle of a room.

Scoring:

3 points if the dog bounds over to you or heads for the door to go out

2 points if the dog comes to you when you walk to the door

1 point if the dog ignores you completely

If your dog has a score of 12 or better, he goes to the front of the class! A score of 8 to 11 means he's of average intelligence. If he scores lower than 8 ... well, just teach him a few awesome tricks, and people will think he's smart!

My Dog Story

"One time I heard my bulldog, Duff, barking and barking. I went to see what was up. It turns out that my hockey stick had fallen across the doorway of the living room. Duff couldn't figure out that he needed to step over it to get out of the room."

—Marcus

Amazing Dogs

Some dogs are smart, and others are extraordinary. Here are stories of amazing dogs that might make you look at your own pooch just a little differently.

• In 2005, dog researchers discovered that a Border collie named Rico understands over 200 words! That is equal to the vocabulary of trained apes, dolphins, and parrots.

• The British medical journal *Lancet* reported that in 1989, a woman went to see a doctor about a mole on her leg. Even though the mark had been there for months and didn't bother her, her dog had recently become obsessed with it, sniffing and licking at it, eventually trying to bite it off. The doctor discovered that the mole was a malignant melanoma, a type of skin cancer that can be deadly. He removed it right away. The dog (a cross between a border collie and a Doberman) may have saved his owner's life!

• When airplanes hijacked by terrorists slammed into the World Trade Center on September 11, 2001, a blind man named Omar Eduardo Rivera was working in his office on the 71st floor. When he realized something horrible was happening, he let his guide dog off the leash so that his beloved companion could escape. But even though he was clearly scared, the golden retriever led Omar to the closest exit and, with the help of Omar's boss, guided him down the stairs to the ground floor. A true hero!

• A German shepherd named Buddha served our country for five years during the Vietnam War. Although he was wounded five times, Buddha protected the lives of many American soldiers and had five confirmed enemy kills in close combat. (And he never complained about the food! What a trouper!)

• The Beagle Brigade works for the U.S. Department of Agriculture. These little dogs, dressed in green uniforms, are trained to sniff around at airports, finding foods that are not allowed to be brought into this country. Each dog can sniff out almost 50 different specific scents, including apple, mango, beef, and pork. This is an important job because the laws banning certain foods protect us from dangerous insects or plant diseases that would harm our food supply.

• In June of 1989, a two-year-old boy named Ernest wandered away from his home in the hills of New Mexico. The family dog, Ivy, was also missing. When Ernest didn't answer their calls, parents James and Angeles Mann called the sheriff who quickly organized a search party.

As the sun went down and the temperature began to drop, the little boy still had not been found. In the morning, 100 searchers were looking for Ernest, but the Manns began to lose hope. Suddenly, a black dog appeared in front of one of the searchers and began gently tugging on his wrist. When the man followed the dog a short distance, he discovered Ernest lying on the ground, asleep between Ivy and another dog.

Weird Dog Fact

The larger a dog's muzzle, the better his sense of smell. So German shepherds smell better than Dachshunds!

The sheriff later said that Ernest would have frozen during the night if Ivy and the two stray dogs hadn't surrounded him and kept him warm.

• When the Hutchinsons moved from New York to Indiana in October of 1988, they left their beagle Oscar with their grandson. They knew that he loved Oscar and would take good care of him.

Oscar, however, clearly missed the Hutchinsons and had his own ideas about where he was going to live. Despite the fact that Oscar had never before been outside of his neighborhood in New York, he left his home and began walking, eventually traveling hundreds of miles, looking for his former owners.

Seven months later, thin and dirty, he appeared at the Hutchinsons' new home. How he found his way there is a complete mystery.

• The first Lassie television show debuted in 1954. Since then, nine dogs have played Lassie, all descendents of the first dog "Pal" from the 1943 movie Lassie Come Home. In 1982, the current Lassie was asked to be a presenter at the Academy Awards. All of the movie stars who attended gave him a standing ovation!

• In China and Japan, dogs are part of the national earthquake warning system. They proved they could be counted on to react to impending earthquakes in 1975 when dogs in the city of Haicheng, China, became very anxious. Based on the dogs' odd behavior, the

Read more amazing dog stories in *Dog Miracles: Inspirational and Heroic True Stories*, by Brad Steiger and Sherry Hansen Steiger.

My Dog Story

"Every day when I come home from school, my chow chow leaps off the front porch and goes charging toward the fence like he's going to jump over it, and then: THUD! He never makes it. But every day he tries it as if it's a completely new idea."

—Sean

officials on earthquake watch evacuated 90,000 people from the city. A few hours later, a huge earthquake struck Haicheng, destroying 90 percent of the buildings there.

• Golden retriever Randi, a certified hearing dog for her deaf owners, will respond to a number of alert sounds including the alarm clock, door bell, smoke alarm, telephone, and sounds of an intruder like a twisting doorknob or a window being raised.

When she hears one of these noises, Randi runs to her owners, Bill and Rhonda Kerr, and stares until they make eye contact. Then she takes them to the source of the sound.

Weird Dog Fact

Dog researchers have determined that dogs can find the source of a sound in 6/100ths of a second.

Randi was trained at a special hearing dog school. She's considered a service dog and is allowed into all public buildings, even those that normally don't allow dogs.

Mad Scientist Experiments

You can do experiments to learn how much you and your dog are alike! Take notes about what you discover.

> ### Experiment #1
>
> *Do dogs "catch" yawns from people the way we do from each other?*

In a quiet room where your dog can see and hear you, yawn loudly. Wait one minute. Did your dog yawn? Try it again, and wait one more minute. (On another day, watch what happens when your dog yawns in a room full of people. Is his yawn contagious? Do the people in the room start to yawn, too?)

_____

_____

_____

My Dog Story

"My Doberman pinscher, Toby, learned that if he pushed a lever on the refrigerator with his nose, ice cubes would come pouring out. He thought it was fun to run around the kitchen sliding on the ice cubes. We tried everything we could think of to block off the refrigerator, but he always found a way to get to it and push the lever. Finally we gave up and decided to replace the refrigerator with one that didn't have an ice dispenser."

—Brian

Experiment #2

Do people's eyes have the same reflective layer behind the retina that dogs' eyes do?

Ask your brother, sister, or a friend to take your dog into a dark room for about five minutes. Step into the room and, from about 20 feet away, shine a flashlight toward them both. What do your dog's eyes look like? Do they glow? What about your friend's eyes?

_____

_____

_____

_____

Experiment #3

Can a dog pick out his owner's scent better than his owner can?

Ask four buddies to bring over one dirty, smelly sock each. Search the hamper and find one of your own. First, tell your friends to place their socks a foot or so apart on the floor. Holding your dog away from the socks, let him smell your sock. Then go place it next to the others. Call him over to the socks and see if he picks yours out!

After that, you have to try the same thing, but blindfolded! Have your friends arrange the socks on the kitchen table. Without touching the socks or being able to see them, sniff each one in turn and then guess which one is yours. Who got it right, you or your dog?

_____

_____

_____

Experiment #4

Who learns better when there are distractions, your friend or your dog?

When you and a friend are watching TV, tell him an interesting fact. About an hour later, ask him if he remembers exactly what you said. Then test your dog's ability to remember something when he's distracted. Bring him into a large room and hide a treat while he watches you—but don't let him go after it. Toss a ball to him for about five minutes, then take him back to the room where the treat is hidden. Does he remember where it is?

_____

_____

_____

Experiment #5

How hard is it for people and dogs to learn new things?

Move the dog's food and water bowls. How long does it take for him to go directly to the new spot without looking in the old spot first? Now move the trash can in the kitchen. How many times do the people in your family go to the wrong spot to throw something away? How long does it take everyone to remember the new location of the trash can?

Experiment #6

Who can figure out the source of a noise more quickly, you or your dog?

Go into the basement or any large area with places to hide things. Think of a noise that always gets your dog's attention, like the sound of you opening a can of food. Have a friend hold your dog on one side of the room while you hide and make the noise. When your friend lets go of the dog, how long will it take him to find you?

Now do the same thing with your friend. Have him stand in the same spot while you hide and make a noise that he responds to, like the sound of a text message coming through on his cell phone. Is he faster at finding you than your dog, or the other way around?

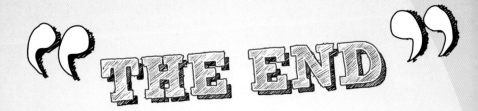
Can you match the ends of these dogs with the breeds?

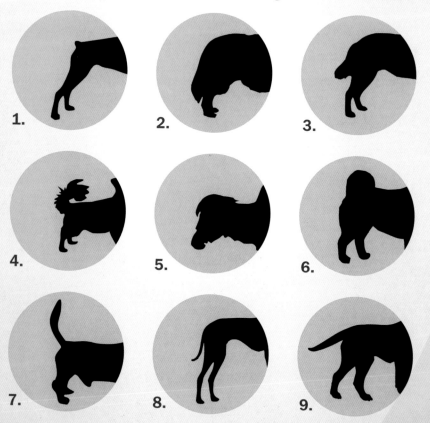

1.

2.

3.

4.

5.

6.

7.

8.

9.

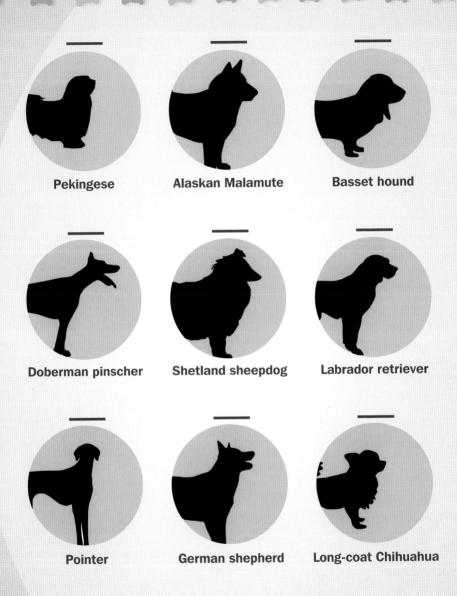

Pekingese

Alaskan Malamute

Basset hound

Doberman pinscher

Shetland sheepdog

Labrador retriever

Pointer

German shepherd

Long-coat Chihuahua

Photo/Illustration Credits

Cover (and throughout) dog bone illustrations, Jimmy Ball; page 5 photo, Carrie Copeland; page 7 photo, John F. Whalen Jr.; page 8 photo, Cynthia Copeland; page 9 boy and dog photo, John F. Whalen Jr.; page 13 baseball photo, Jimmy Ball; page 23 photo, Jimmy Ball; page 24 photo, John F. Whalen Jr.; page 26 baby gate and crate illustrations, Jimmy Ball; page 27 leash photo, Jimmy Ball; page 42-43 all illustrations, Jimmy Ball; page 49 photo, John F. Whalen Jr.; page 60 photo, John F. Whalen Jr.; page 80 photo, John F. Whalen Jr.; pages 82-83 illustration, Cynthia Copeland; page 89 illustration, Cynthia Copeland; page 100 photo, John F. Whalen Jr.; page 113 illustration, Cynthia Copeland; pages 116-117 illustration, Cynthia Copeland; page 123 all images Jimmy Ball; page 152 illustration, Cynthia Copeland.

Colophon

Publisher: John F. Whalen Jr.
Author: Cynthia Copeland
Editor: Arliss Paddock
Cover/interior design: Jimmy Ball
Print management: Imago USA
Distribution: Simon & Schuster

This book was designed on an Apple®
MacBook Pro using Adobe InDesign
CS3. The fonts used for this book are
Franklin Gothic ITC; book, **demi** and
italic faces for the body copy are set
12/14. 14 pt. and 12 pt. **Sketch
Rockwell** is used for the headers and
subheads respectively.